Beyond the Natural

Beyond the Natural

by
Chacko Thomas

Exciting experiences, stories and lessons from seeing
God at work in about 100 nations when serving in India,
Logos, Doulos, Logos II and now based in the United
Kingdom with Operation Mobilisation (OM)

SPM
Special Projects
Ministries

Beyond the Natural
by Chacko Thomas

Copyright © 2011, Chacko Thomas

ISBN: 9780955841279
First edition
Reprint 2011

Published by
Special Project Ministries (A Ministry of OM International)
P.O. Box 660
Forest Hill, London SE 23 3ST
United Kingdom

Printed and bound in India by
Authentic Media, Secunderabad 500 067, A.P. India
e-mail: printing@ombooks.org

Endorsements:

This is an incredible, passionate and candid account of a person's journey with God. It's moving and filled with details of God's extraordinary work through an ordinary man that took him from India to minister in about 100 nations for the cause of the Gospel. It illustrates the truth of what God can do with a man who is sold out for him.
Rev Dr Mark Chua (Malaysia)
Methodist Hokkien Church, Kuala Lumpur

This book made me laugh out loud and also brought tears to my eyes. I think you will find the same. Some of the stories will stay in your mind for days afterwards, as the Lord teaches you from them. Anyone with a heart to learn from the Lord will find much here to feed their spirit. I wish I could have read it years ago!
Dr. Grace Marshall (United Kingdom)
Medical Doctor

I have watched personally and up close as Chacko Thomas has walked with Christ through the rigors of pioneer evangelism in the villages of India, the demands of leadership on ocean-going ships manned by Christians from many nations, and the trauma of deep family loss. His life radiates the grace and wisdom decades of obedience to the Son of God form within. This account is rich with examples; may it serve as a beacon for many!
George Miley (USA)
Founder, Antioch Network
International Fellowship of Christians Preparing the Way for the Lord.
General Director, OM Ships International (1972-1985)

A thrilling, easy-to read account of one who responds, constrained by the love of God, to the call to stay open to the Lord for Him to lead, in the midst of intense struggle in spiritual warfare against the forces of darkness. A breathtaking story of deliverance, during the 60-year journey with God, together with many brothers and sisters in the Lord from many different nations.

P. Abraham, (India)
Editor, Light of Life
The Magazine for Christian Growth

It is a joy that Chacko put some of his thoughts and stories on paper. May God use these to encourage more disciples of Christ. This book is practical, real, honest, funny at times but a proof of God at work in our lives. I continue to thank God for bringing many mentors into my life but Chacko Thomas continues to be my hero. Not that he is perfect but open, honest and quick to repent and led me by model. I appreciated him. May the Lord use his book for stirring your heart.

K. Rajendran, (India)
A continuous learner,
Global Roundtables of Innovation & Leadership Development,
Chairman - World Evangelical Alliance Mission Commission

Chacko Thomas has been a friend and fellow-servant for over thirty years. When I first joined the Doulos, Chacko was one of the directors. His life and ministry have spoken deeply into the lives of so many of us in Latin America. Still today, as I travel and meet some of those ministry friends in many countries, Chacko's name will pop up to our minds and we will reflect on how God has mightily used him to teach His word and challenge believers in our part of the world to a life of commitment to Christ and the Great Commission. His testimony, shared in these pages, has stirred my heart again to be an obedient and trustworthy disciple and disciple maker. Thank you Chacko, for your dedication, humility and your love for God, His people and the lost!

Decio de Carvalho (Brazil)
Executive Director
COMIBAM Internacional

Interesting, eventful and meaningful account of what God can do in and through a believer who is committed and available to Him. Much time with God and the Scriptures were important in equipping and enabling brother Chacko to fulfil what the Lord desired of him.
Lim Kou (Singapore)
Author and Elder of Christian Ekklesia,

When George Miley and I were on the OM ship Logos in the early days we often discussed about people with potential that we might be able to recruit to help us in the ministry of the ship. Chacko's name often came up for discussion, but to recruit him out of India seemed impossible. Chacko excelled in all of the different roles that he was thrown into and was used mightily by God. Reading through Chacko's account of his life-especially in OM we not only have an account of God taking this earthly vessel and using it for His glory, but through Chacko's eyes also a history of OM. I am sure that you will be blessed as well as challenged in reading this account.
Frank Dietz, (USA)
Minister-at-large, OM International

It was in 1988-90 aboard MV Doulos that I got to know Chacko Thomas. He was then Associate Director of this ship with international staff and crew giving or committing 2 years of their lives to serve on board and serve the nations. Seeing and hearing Chacko, I see and feel his deep love for the Lord and passion for people. It was such a blessing to serve directly under his leadership even for a short stint before I was to finish my commitment. Since then until today, I am in touch with him, a man who loves the Lord dearly.
Jun Diaz, (The Philippines)
Director, Operation Mobilisation - Philippines.

The first time I met Chacko was in Bihar, north India in 1983. He left an impression on me then and continues to until today. I fondly refer to him as Chackocha (older brother). What others will say of the man I know I will echo and his works for the Kingdom of God are evident

here... Chacko would be considered unsuccessful by the world's standard... He is a man of God in the true sense of the word. He has a surrendered heart, is transparent, is a lover of God, who waits for God, a lover of the Word, a lover of people and a good friend.
Shankar Sankannavar, Northern Ireland

Chacko and Radha with their children rejoined the ship Doulos in 1990. My wife Annagret and I lived onboard with our children, and I was the Personnel Manager. Chacko was the Associate Director. I so much appreciated working under his co-leadership with Bernd Gülker. Chacko's ministry to the ship's community of more than 300 people from over 40 different nations was invaluable. He was setting an example as a leader who always took an active part in prayer meetings, preaching and teaching the Word. Many recruits onboard experienced personal discipleship from him as a leader who took a real interest in their lives and development.
Andreas Schafer (Germany)
Personnel Director, OM Ships International

As a nephew of uncle Chacko, it is an honour to write about him. Among all his characteristics, his simplicity and dedication for God's work all over the world stand tall in his life. His book "Beyond the Natural," comes out at a very right time. His life and vast experiences in life and ministry reflected in the pages of this book would really encourage and challenge God's people and ministers, especially young ministers like me, to live for Christ in this hostile-looking world. I recommend this book to every Christian, especially those who are engaged in ministry. May God use this book to bless many.
Rev. Finny Abraham
Senior Pastor, Dua Ka Ghar,
Meerut, UP, India

God's power is manifested through our weaknesses! Chacko's openness, brokenness and humility forms a powerful backdrop against which God could paint His story of faith, love and commitment through

his servant. May you be blessed and built up in your faith, as I was, to trust God in new ways to see His fame spread through all the earth.
Francois Vosloo
Director, OM Southern Africa,
Associate International Director, OM International

Chacko Thomas has given us personal dimensions of the beginnings of the modern Indian missionary movement in the 1960's and 70's. Chacko has himself given lifelong leadership to the majority world participation in the Great Commission. I highly recommend this volume.
Dave and Cathy Hicks (USA)
Founder, AlongSideAsia: *Partnering Coaching Teaching,*
OM India & OM Ships (1967-1980) OM Coordinator for US and N. America (1980-2000), President, Bethany International (2001-2006)

Dedicated to

The Living Triune God
Father, Son and Holy Spirit
The great Creator, Ruler, Sustainer, Redeemer and Judge
Loving, gracious, just and righteous
The Almighty
My Lord and my God
Deeply grateful for His patient and gracious working in and through
His unworthy servant

Two Pastors
Pastor K.P Oommen and Rev. Dr. Quek Swee Hwa
And their congregations

Three Mentors
George Verwer, George Miley and Frank Dietz
From whom I have learned much

Four of my Heroes
Parents: Mr and Mrs AC Thomas
Brother: Joseph Thomas
Sister: Mrs Mariamma Abraham

And
Three fellow-soldiers
Wife: Radha (Nair) Thomas
Daughter: Sheela J Thomas
Son: Sunil Thomas (1985-2003)

Contents:

CONTENTS

Foreword

Be warned, dear readers, this is no ordinary book. You can follow the accounts with curiosity as the fascinating stories it contains unfold. Or, if you can identify yourself personally with some of the people and places mentioned in this book, you will perhaps like me find it very hard to put it down once you have started reading the journey of faith that our dear brother Chacko has taken us. And you will be shaken with the realization that when God is at work in a person's life or in a ministry blessed by Him, things are bound to happen "beyond the natural," beyond our wildest expectation!

Reading this book was one huge, heart-wrenching, cathartic experience for me. This is primarily a personal recollection of the many, diverse situations in Chacko's varied life and ministry. The Lord has indeed used him greatly to spread the Gospel far and wide. But beyond the autobiographical reflections, this is a book about a work that was dear to his heart. Like many of the leaders of OM, Chacko's life and the history of OM are intertwined. We have one more of the many books that tell the story of whole spectrum of OM's work. We can discern clearly God's hand of guidance and blessing on a ministry that has touched many, many lives all over the world. The accounts are narrated with candour and sometimes with reserve, particularly in the description of Sunil's promotion to glory. We get the impression that there is still some deep-seated healing that needs to take place. We hope the writing of this book and the good reception it is bound to receive will help Chacko, Radha and Sheela find complete peace in God's work in their family.

It is my joy to recommend this book to everyone. The Apostle Paul, referring to Isa 64:4, wrote these beautiful words in 1 Cor. 2:9, "Eye hath not seen, nor ear heard, neither have entered into the heart of man, the things which God hath prepared for them that love him." Thank God we can discover in our lives the surpassing riches and glory of God. Hear Paul again, who stated: "For I reckon that the sufferings of this present time are not worthy to be compared with the glory which shall be revealed in us" (Rom.8:18).

Rev Dr Quek Swee Hwa
Senior Pastor, Zion B-P Church (1975-2007), Singapore
Senior Pastor-at-Large & Missions Director,
Zion Bishan B-P Church, Singapore
Founder: Biblical Graduate School of Theology, Singapore

A sleepless night

London, July 2009. It was an unusual night. Normally I sleep well. But here I was lying awake in bed for hours, reflecting on the past 60 years of my life. It may have been triggered off by the 60th birthday party that Radha, my wife, and Sheela, my daughter, had planned for me for the next evening. Reflecting on the years in about 100 countries all over the globe in all kinds of circumstances was a God-given experience. He brought many people, places and incidents to mind.

Imagine, for example, the shock of a grenade going off just eight feet behind you when you are preaching to hundreds of people in front of you. Then the surprise that you came away from it all, absolutely unhurt although not a little shaken up by the events around you. Then the relief that the second grenade that rolled under your platform did not go off. This was in 1991 when I served with the OM ship Doulos. It was gracious God sparing my life, again.

"You guys live in the supernatural" was the comment of a missionary who once visited us on the Doulos; after observing what God was doing in and through the Doulos team. Truly, there is a supernatural dimension to life. It is because the living and true God is personally and constantly involved in our lives.

I have many stories and experiences of God to share with you. These are not only stories of God's gracious work in and through my life but also the stories of many others who have invested in my life.

God knew exactly what He was doing, although I had little idea of what I was getting into, when I left home 44 years ago on that October 10th in 1966. I have been swept into and been part of a spiritual revolution God was bringing about in our time. Thank you Lord Jesus. It is a great privilege to be able to participate in an adventure of knowing God and making Him known.

To God be the glory

Chacko Thomas,
Minister-at-large
OM Special Projects
P.O.Box 660
Forest Hill,
London SE23 3SH.
UNITD KINGDOM
chacko.thomas@om.org

Early Experiences of God

I was born on 17th July 1949 in Kerala, in India. The hospital where I was born is still there, but of course the standard of health-care it offers is much better than what it used to be 60 years ago. The house I was raised in is also still there; my younger brother (being the youngest) inherited it according to our culture. I was the firstborn of my parents, nine years after their marriage.

At the time of my birth, my parents were new believers, worshipping with the Brethren Assemblies. But in a few years they moved over to the Indian Pentecostal Church. It was a Pentecostal fellowship with a strong Brethren influence. Prayer and the Word of God were strongly emphasised. These strands of spiritual influences were helpful for a vibrant faith. Three things stand out in my recollection of the 1950s that have a bearing on my future.

A prophetic word? I was about four years old, at a weekly prayer meeting. Everybody sat in a circle on mats on the floor, and I was sleeping on the mat next to my father. Suddenly I woke up, fully awake and saw a man at the other end of the circle, on his knees and moving towards my father. He told my father, in my hearing, while pointing at me: "This boy will go all over the world and preach the gospel before Jesus returns." I heard it as clear as a bell. My parents never talked about it. But it has been impressed in my memory. Of course, I did not know what it meant then. Looking back now, I would still say I was an extremely unlikely candidate.

A living God who speaks? My maternal grandmother was a nominal Christian, but came to a personal faith during her old age. The way she died had an impact on me. She died just as the Lord had revealed to her - on the specific day and at the precise hour. She had been ill and living in our home for a few weeks to enable my mother to look after her. At her request, my parents brought her back to her own house because she wanted to die in her own home. My mother went to stay with her to look after her.

As my father was saying good-bye to grandmother, I heard her saying to my father, "Be back here before 4 pm, Thursday, next week." She also told my mother: "There will be many people here on Thursday afternoon. Be prepared to receive them." Sure enough, she passed away at the time she said she would, with all the family standing by her bed and my mother praying. And mother had prepared refreshments for the visitors. This was an experience that would often come to my mind. The Lord and the realities in the spiritual realm were becoming real to me.

Psalm 16 is the only passage I can recall reading during my early years. I read it over and over. I have always thought it was a psalm the Lord gave me, although I did not know why I thought that. Now, as I look back over my life, having seen the way the Lord has preserved me both physically and spiritually, the good fellowship I have had with so many saints from all over the world, all the pleasant places I have been to, the Lord's counsel, the joy of the Lord - I see clearly the relevance of Psalm 16 to my life.

School days I had to walk nearly a mile, with my friends to go to primary school. It was quite safe in those days. What I remember from those schooldays is that I was commended for my grasp of (basic) English. I also did well in my mother tongue, Malayalam. It was helpful I came from that part of Kerala where people spoke good Malayalam. I did not do too badly in basic Hindi. All these three languages were needful for my subsequent preaching ministry. I still make use of them in my ministry. As a point of interest: the word "MALAYALAM" can be read backwards or forwards. We like to say that this is the language used in heaven - because it takes an eternity to learn it!

Early exposure to the Christian faith The Sunday school at church was run like formal classes in schools - with exams and grades, all the way to the 10th grade, which I completed by about age 16. I owe a lot to my Sunday school, although at that time I was in two minds about it - especially with regards to all the memorisation I had to do - of Bible verses and names of the apostles and patriarchs and the names of the books of the Bible. But that was the right age to memorise these things. The school also provided incentives, including competitions and presents.

Besides the Sunday school, very able Bible teachers and preachers, who were knowledgeable and passionate, preached clear messages from the Scriptures during the Sunday services and the church's yearly evangelistic rallies, known as "conventions." During the yearly convention seasons, there were a variety of messages we could choose to listen to. Joy Oommen, the pastor's son and I, in our teenage years, would travel several miles to get to listen to various speakers.

Salvation was the main theme of the messages. Pastor P.M. Philip (now with the Lord) was at his best when preaching on the crucifixion of the Lord Jesus Christ. I can see him dressed all in white, walking back and forth on the stage, with tears rolling down his cheeks, and explaining the fulfilment of Isaiah 53 in our Lord. Another speaker, Pastor T.G Oommen, was at His best when preaching from the book of Hebrews. These men knew their Bibles thoroughly. There were many godly pioneers in those days. We left those meetings fully awakened, in our souls and spirits. The messages were long, but often broken into parts by spontaneous singing in response to what was being preached.

The main convention (gospel rally) for me was the one in our church, just across the street from home. It was a festival-like atmosphere with a loud generator for the many florescent lights, loudspeaker system and for playing the gospel songs from records. These songs, played on

19

maximum volume, will start an hour before the convention, to get all in the vicinity to come. Some of these songs were sufficient in themselves to help people know the gospel. A family recently presented me with a leather bound Malayalam song book with over a 1000 old and new songs in it. It dawned on me what God had been communicating to me in those years through these songs. The songs were Bible truths put to music. There was a strong emphasis on God as the Creator and Redeemer, as well as the eager anticipation of the Second Coming of Christ and heaven. The theme of worship as recorded in Revelation is strongly echoed.

Conversion In 1962 at age 13, I confessed my sins to the Lord Jesus Christ and asked Him to come into my heart to be my Lord and Saviour. I committed myself to follow Him, and He has sustained me all these years. Many things contributed to my salvation, not least the sincere faith of my parents – expressed in the way they lived out their lives. But it was one of the Gospel tracts from the stack my father had bought and kept in the house (for distribution) that helped me take the decisive step.

The leaflet was entitled "Five wounds of Christ". It was based on Isaiah 53:5 and Romans 8:1. "But He was pierced through for our transgressions, He was crushed for our iniquities; The chastening for our well-being fell upon Him, And by His scourging we are healed" (Isa. 53:5). "Therefore there is now no condemnation for those who are in Christ Jesus" (Rom. 8:1). The tract went on to say: "But as many as received Him, to them He gave the right to become children of God, even to those who believe in His name" (John 1:12). Its message was clear as crystal to me. I knew that Christ died in my place for my sins. And His death was sufficient for the forgiveness of my sins and for my salvation.

Only one thing remained - I must personally acknowledge the truth of the Gospel and invite the living Lord Jesus Christ into my life. So I knelt down in my room and told the Lord Jesus Christ, "Lord, I believe it is my sins that put you on the cross, I am a sinner, please forgive me my sins, please come into my heart and be my saviour. Make me your child, and I want to follow you from this day forward." I got up from my knees believing that the Lord Jesus Christ had heard me and accepted me. I had become a child of God. I had been born again.

Nothing extraordinary in the visible realm took place then, but something marvellous was taking place in the spiritual realm, in my heart and in my relationship with God – because I believed and responded positively to what was recorded in the Scriptures. Since that moment, I have known an abiding presence of God with me all my life. I have never been alone.

Open air preaching. I started joining the church's weekly open-air meetings on Sunday afternoons, in villages and small towns nearby. My role was distributing tracts, which my father had kept in the house, bought from a tract society in Kottayam. What a ministry this tract society was, in enabling us to be a voice for the Lord. I also participated in shouting out loud Bible verses like John 3:16, as we walked past homes on our way to preach. We could see people stopping whatever they were doing in the field and listening to us.

Strangely, these verses which I was sharing with others were working more deeply in my own life, although I was not so conscious of it till later. They convicted me that all mankind are lost in sin and Jesus is the only way out. I would recommend believers to memorise these verses: John 1:12, 3:16, 3:3, 14:6; Romans 3:23, 6:23; Acts 16:31, 4:12; 1 Tim 1:15, Rev 3:20, 1 Peter 1:24, 25 and Eph. 2:8-9. It is vital that the meaning of these verses reach deep into our hearts. The world needs to know them too.

Once, in an open-air meeting in a small town called Ayarkunnam, about three miles from my home, I was standing on the front row and singing along with the group. The pastor, (K.P.Oommen), stood in the last row, being the tallest person in church. He was expected to preach at the end of the song. Half way through the song, with no warning at all, he tapped me on the shoulder from behind and said, "You speak first and then I will speak." I guess I was too scared to say no. I had never done anything like this.

I opened my New Testament and it fell opened on Revelation 20. The verses about the Great White Throne Judgement (verses 11-15) caught my eyes. I quickly read the few verses and I felt I understood them - they became the theme of my first message. I must have heard many sermons on them. My voice was not loud enough, and so an older gentleman, a passionate speaker himself, repeated my words after me, so everyone could hear. It is like translation during preaching, a sentence or a phrase at a time, except in this case what was repeated was in the same language. This was how the Lord put me on the road to preaching, on the spot. I guess, we are supposed to be ready to preach, in season and out of season (2 Tim 4:2)!

Near miss with a huge viper. The rule in our home was that we should all be home before dark. Kerala villages in the evening became very dark and very quickly, partly because of the many huge tropical trees. We had no streetlights in those days. Even in our homes and in the many villages nearby, there was no electricity. I was raised on kerosene lamps and my mother used wood for cooking. Electricity and gas came many years later.

One evening, I walked home in the dark. I was nearing home. Only a few steps remained before I would turn left to go up the few steps to my house. As I was about to lift my right foot up for the next step, a very mild light shone around me for a split second. And I saw, right in front of me, a very big snake heading towards my house. My next step would have been on its tail. Quietly and scared, I went home and told my father. He immediately took the stick which was specially kept for killing snakes, and also lit a couple of readymade bundles of coconut palm leaves for use as a torch (both were readily available in most homes in Kerala) and went down to kill the snake.

For a while the snake could not be found. Then someone spotted it half way up the stonewall heading into our property. The snake being in this position made it easier for my father to kill it. However, my father who was a strong man had to hit the snake on the head three times before it fell to the ground. He then killed it. It was a huge viper. This was one of the many occasions the Lord preserved my life.

1964, baptism at age 15. I was not baptised as a child, as my parents were Brethren.

I obeyed the Lord in water baptism along with a few others in a small river a short walk from church. The whole church walked in a procession and sang as they walked. Imagine all of them dressed in white - men, women and many children. One of the songs sung at my baptism can be found in many languages. It was one of the few songs in those days translated into Malayalam from English:

O Happy day! that fixed my choice

On Thee, my Saviour and my God;
Well may this glowing heart rejoice,
And tell its raptures all abroad.

Chorus: Happy day, happy day,
   When Jesus washed my sins away!
   He taught me how to watch and pray;
   And live rejoicing every day.
   Happy day, happy day,
      When Jesus washed my sins away!

Holy Communion and the Holy Kiss. I began to partake of the Lord's Supper. It was truly "in remembrance" of the Lord, in an unhurried way, with freedom for all to share, as led by the Lord, mostly in reading relevant passages from the Scriptures about the death of Christ or songs on the same theme. The church service always ended with the Lord's Table and a "Holy Kiss" on the cheeks, men among themselves and women among themselves. We were in church from 9.00 am till 1pm, beginning with Sunday school and ending with the church service.

Mrs. K.P Oommen, the elderly widow of the pastor, recently commented to me when she recalled those days: "What love there was among the people!" The brethren were dwelling together in love and harmony irrespective of all differences. Is there a better indication of the presence of the Holy Spirit and that we are filled with the Holy Spirit than love and harmony among us? Can anything else take its place in a church? Is not love a major theme in the Bible? It has a prominent place in the Gospels and the epistles. Love should be considered as one of the main teachings (doctrines) of the Bible.

My mother promoted to Glory. 1966, January 23, my mother passed away, at age 39. I was 16, my sister just 13 and my brother just 7 years old. Our father took good care of us, especially my sister and brother, as I was away most of the year. The influence of our parents on all three of us was very strong. Those who knew them appreciated and respected them. We children felt very honoured. Our mum taught us to respect our father, by example as well as insisting that we did. We always had to rise up when he came home. We also had to rise up for anyone who was their age or older (Leviticus 19: 3, 32).

I still do not understand why God took my mother away. She was a key person in the family, church and neighbourhood and she was a woman who prayed much. From what I can observe, my parents had a great marriage. It seems to me they never had a quarrel or a major disagreement. They lived for the Lord and raised us up for the Lord to the best of their ability. I only remember one caning from my father. It was because my mother overheard me "name calling" my sister. It was just one word I heard that day at school and I thought I would try it out on my sister. My mum did not say anything till dad came home in the evening. She took my hand and gave it to him together with a cane, and she said, "ask him what he called his sister." My dad gave me three strokes of the cane, which was enough to stop me going down that road again. Mum taught the three of us to love and respect one another. Our parents also taught us to fear the Lord. God was always in the picture.

At home on Sundays, we had to wait until all the visitors had eaten before we could have our lunch. These were people who had walked a long distance to come to the church which was near our house, and mum felt that she had to feed them (a simple meal) before their journey home. I guess it was also to encourage them in their faith. As their numbers grew, they formed their own (two) churches, and thus need not take the long walk.

A word from the Lord? It took place during our church's fasting and prayer week, an annual event where a few fasted and all attended the evening revival meetings. There was a lady who did not know my family, having recently moved into our area with her husband and children. During one of the breaks between prayer sessions she said to me, "I was praying for you and the Lord gave me Isaiah 43 to give to you." She then read the first seven verses and explained its meaning. She said that the Lord was calling me to serve Him all over the world, pointing to verses 5 and 6:

5 "Do not fear, for I am with you;
I will bring your offspring from the east,
And gather you from the west.
6 "I will say to the north, 'Give them up!'
And to the south, 'Do not hold them back.'
Bring My sons from afar
And My daughters from the ends of the earth,

She mentioned I would travel by ships and planes. I must confess what she said did not have an impact on me, it made no sense. Her words to me were like water off a duck's back. At that time, even to get on board a bus was a luxury for me. However, what she said to me began to unfold over the next forty years of my life, not long after she said it. That lady is now with the Lord, but the gentleman who said something similar about 12 years earlier is still alive, even as I write this book. He is also the one who assisted me with my first preaching in the open air. We must be wary of the many false prophets but God can still give His servants the gift of prophecy. May the Lord continue to gift His servants as He sees fit.

Bible School. I was at a short term Bible School, studying at the feet of some great pioneers like Pastor PM Philip, Pastor T.G. Oommen and Pastor T. P Varughese. These men knew their Bibles backwards and forwards and have suffered much for the faith. A team from Operation Mobilisation India (OM) visited the Bible School. One of the team members, T I Thomas from Kottayam, challenged me to join OM to evangelise "those who have never once heard John 3:16 for the first time in their lives". Actually it was more direct than that. He asked: "What are you doing for the millions of people who have never heard John 3:16 for the first time in their lives?" I was taken aback that a total stranger would talk to me like that.

We had quite an argument, as I was sure that no such people existed in India, as was the case from the part of Kerala I came from. I thought all India was like it. He said, "Come, and you will see." I was put in touch with the state leader of OM, A.G. Philip, a college lecturer in his forties who had resigned from his job to join OM. He and his wife ran the OM office, based in Trivandrum, the capital of the state. They had only one team in the state. They were operating in Eranakulam, north of Kottayam, my district. OM was unheard of in those days. I secured my father's permission to join OM for six months. He wanted me to go to a Bible College in Bangalore after the six months. I had recently turned 17 years.

Joined OM (October 10, 1966). I was one of the three new recruits joining OM that day in Eranakulam, together with N.J. Varughese and M.Paulose. The team leader was Frank Dietz, an American about age 27. Also on the team were Billy Jones, an ex- boxer, Doug Nichols and Ian Farr. Thomas Samuel, the All India Co-ordinator of OM. George Miley, then PA to George Verwer, joined us for a short while. They came to assist Frank Dietz with preaching, it being the convention season in Kerala.

During the day we would go out into the town to conduct open air preaching and sell Gospel portions. For the first day of outreach I was given two large bundles of Gospel portions, with a hundred Gospel portions in each bundle. The team's method of operation helped to draw me out of my shell. We had to sell these Gospels to make money for our food.

When the report of what I was doing got home, some people told my father that I was not truly in the ministry. To them, only preaching counted - and I was not preaching. I was selling Gospel portions on street corners! I will never know what my father thought of it himself, or how he handled it. Maybe he did not give it much thought because to him, it was only for six months, and then I would be home. I thank God for my pastor who prayed for me regularly every Sunday at the close of the service. Only eternity would reveal the significance of those prayers. I am still in OM - after 44 years.

Bangalore, December 1966. Within two months of joining the team, the three of us new recruits were sent to Bangalore in preparation for cross-cultural evangelism. It was not a great start for me. A few days after I got there I was down with chicken pox. I was sent into a special hospital, so that others on our team wouldn't be infected. Finally I was discharged and returned to the OM base in time for the closing night of the OM orientation conference held under a colourful tent. George Verwer, the founder of OM, about 28 years old then, had already started speaking. We did not actually meet, until a few years later. I had no idea of the impact he was to have on my entire future, first indirectly through the OM training, and subsequently, through working together.

A. Stephen. One event during the Bangalore days that has been imprinted into my memory was what happened to A. Stephen. Stephen was in one of the teams and he was taken by a mob of Hindu fanatics to the police station. This was new for me. Stephen was a Hindu convert from Tamil Nadu. Although young, about my age, he was a dynamic speaker and bold for the Lord. I felt very upset. Why should they do this to Stephen? We have come to give them the good news. They should be glad that people have come to help them. I was ready to go home. Yes, I had a lot to learn. I thank God that it was only much later that I personally encountered opposition. The Lord knew I was not ready for it. We all came together to pray for his release. Stephen returned safely and the experience only made him bolder for the Lord. We served many years together in North India. Interestingly, he now lives in Bangalore and impacting all India through his evangelistic literature and church planting ministries.

K.P Yohannan was another zealous young man. He used to carry a flag on a long pole. The flag had different colours on it and he used it for preaching the Gospel in the open air. The black colour stood for sin, to show that we are sinners. Red represented the blood of Christ, white for cleansing and being made righteous, green for growth in the faith and gold for heaven. One day I heard that someone was very upset that he used black for sin. The man said, "What do you mean by black is for sin? Look at my wife. She is black but she is an angel!"

One Saturday evening we were playing Volley Ball. I got very angry with someone and it spoiled the game. I went out of the gate for a walk. When I came back it was dark, and I could hear a few people praying. I recognised Yohannan's voice. He was praying for me, that "God would give me victory over my anger". That was the first time I recognised that my anger was offensive to God and that it is sin. God heard their prayer and He helped me manage my anger from that time onwards. It was evident to me that God was at work in me. The great work of K.P Yohannan for the advancement of the Kingdom through Gospel for Asia is well known.

OM leadership N.J. Varughese, M. Paulose and I were under the leadership of Putturaj from Karnataka state, of which Bangalore is the capital. He and A. Stephen were the first Hindu Background Believers (HBBs), or as a friend of mine, also from Hindu background prefers to call them: "First Generation Followers of Christ", I have ever met. Their number has grown since those days and many of them are now leading the work of God in India.

We were under the supervision of the OM All India Co-ordinator Thomas Samuel, who co-ordinated OM India from Bangalore. Thomas Samuel and his wife Marykutty looked after us like parents would. Thomas Samuel has the distinction of being the first Indian OMer. George Verwer had requested Union Biblical Seminary in India, to send two students to take part in the large OM summer campaign in Europe, and Thomas Samuel was one of the two. After observing George and the OM work in the summer of 1963 he regularly prayed,

'Lord please send George and OM to India'. Finally he felt it is time to talk to George. But it was George who sent for him to talk about India. God's timing is perfect.

North India, here we come. Thomas Samuel took the risk of sending me, N.J. Varughese and M. Paulose to join OM teams at the other end of India; in Bihar State, right below Nepal. Bihar was known as "the graveyard of missions" because of the poor response and the terrible opposition to the preaching of the Gospel. We travelled the OM way, in the back of an OM truck, driven by Ian Farr, an Englishman. The OM truck needed to leave the country and come back in as required by the law.

When we were near the India Nepal border, Ian decided to do open air preaching in order to sell the small stock of Hindi Gospel portions we had. I do not remember the details of how I ended up "translating" for him. I certainly had more zeal than knowledge, but we did manage to sell some Gospel portions. Eventually we joined the OM work in the OM region of "North East India", consisting of the four states of Bihar, Bengal, U.P and Orissa. I became part of a men's travelling team, although we were called "the Boys teams".

My first job in the team was "Literature Man". Other team positions were: Team leader, Finance Man, Team Driver and Team members. I was responsible for two to three tons of Christian literature stored at the back of the large OM truck for the team to distribute. This was meant to be the supply for a month, as the demand was good. Sometimes we would sell out half-way through the month and we would have to drive back to the team base to restock.

We were glad to see such large numbers of Gospel portions being sold to the non-Christian public. The sale and distribution of the literature always preceded the open air singing and preaching. We would usually spend five to eight hours daily in this routine, with short breaks for lunch. One catch was that we had to sell to get the money to eat, being volunteers and earning no salaries. Like it or not we had to learn to sell Gospel literature, and many team members learned to excel in their ability to sell. This practice drew me out of my shell. The income was used for fuel, repair of the vehicle and any other team expenses like medical needs. The excess amount was sent to the OM base to help out with the operations there. Some of it was recycled into more literature.

An India I never knew existed. The physical and spiritual needs of Bihar seem to show up together. I knew the answer was the Lord Jesus Christ. A passion for the lost, from God, was taking hold of me. In the words of the apostle Paul: "the love of Christ constrained me". I had found my reason for living – which is more than mere existence. It was three years before I went home – way past the six months I agreed with my father. And the time at home lasted only two weeks. A timely letter came from Ron Penny, the regional leader, encouraging me to return to Bihar - and I did.

Five to eight hours a day, standing around in street corners in the hot sun or the bitter cold of the winter preaching Christ and distributing the endless supply of tracts and selling Gospel literature was not a chore. Often there was opposition, at times life threatening - like being stoned or beaten. It was not stress free, but we slept well - even though it was often by the road side or riverbed.

Occasionally, we were fortunate to find a church building to stay in or to enjoy the hospitality of Christians. I remember a Christian couple feeding the team of 14 of us for a month - breakfasts before we set out for the day's work, and evening meals on our return to stay with them. They were both doctors, Lewis and Hannah Williams from Madras, now Chennai. On one occasion our discussion turned to the subject of their saving up for the rainy day. Dr. Lewis said, "We have better use for the money." By this he meant investing in the Kingdom. The couple subsequently served the Lord in Afghanistan, their first love.

Our teams all over India would distribute 12 million pieces of Gospel literature a year. This included Gospel tracts. Being in north India was being among many "millions of people who have never heard John 3:16 for the first time in their life" and doing something about it – just as T.I Thomas challenged me not so long ago. Oh, I am so glad that God let me have a part in it. Thank you Lord Jesus. I am still deeply convicted that one of the greatest needs in India today is for all its inhabitants to read at least one Gospel, know who the Lord Jesus is and what He has done for them. Who will tell them of the love of Jesus?

In God's School in North India

God was with us and working in our midst. The team motto was: "To Know Christ and to Make Him Known". We were growing in our knowledge of God in the situations we go through, and God was revealing Himself to us, especially through the way He answered our prayers. It became increasingly clear to me that it was more important to God that I grow in my knowledge of Him, than all I could do for Him or humanity. Sharing one's faith with non-Christians is a great way to know the Lord, and to grow in Him. And it brings much joy.

We worked as a team. And that was the secret of our not giving up. Team life had many advantages. Safety, boldness, making a bigger impact than going at it alone, motivation to press on, discipline and encouragement, correcting and learning from one another and praying together are some of the advantages. I was in the company of some great people, including Billy Jones (now with the Lord), Ron Penny, John Hymus, A Stephen, George Miley, Dave and Cathy Hicks, Chris Begg (now with the Lord), Mike Wakely, and Ebenezer Sunderaj. What an influence these men had on my life! Fire is caught not taught.

We had a large number of British and Americans on our teams. We were learning disciplines from them no amount of messages would have taught us. Of course they were learning a thing or two from us Indians too. Their commitment to truth, keeping time, sacrifice, hard work, openness, straight forwardness and many more were contagious.

I could write a page on each of them. In fact five years ago (2006), I wrote a book on one of them, Billy Jones the boxer.

Billy Jones the boxer. He was a champion boxer from Great Britain. He was so good at it, that out of a hundred boxing matches he only lost four matches, and only by points. No one had been able to knock him out. But he was a gentleman - of course you do not want to upset a champion boxer. He came to know the Lord late in life, after a long search for the true God. This included three talks with Mahatma Gandhi.

He was no longer young when he joined Christian Missions. He met up with young George Verwer, the Founder and International Co-Coordinator of Operation Mobilisation, who has been big into making exceptions to the rules and taking risks. Billy became an OMer at age 52, while I became one at age 17.

Eventually Billy came to India. This was not his first visit to India. He had travelled all over India during the World War II to fight for the British Empire. But this time he was here on a greater mission, for the King of Kings. Billy was just what India needed. He had to speak through a translator, but he was the team's favourite Open Air preacher. People loved to hear this white man, all muscles, with a huge chest and heavy hands and thick fingers, but with a gentle look on his face. He spoke as though he was back in a boxing ring. It was interesting watching him. His whole body spoke. But what he had to say was even more amazing.

He often spoke about his long and unsuccessful search for God which included talking three times to India's Mahatma Gandhi, and how Gandhi could not help him find God. He spoke to many priests and bishops, and they were equally unhelpful. One day he was handed a leaflet entitled: "You have tried the devil's way long enough - try God's way". In five minutes the leaflet showed him how to find God. He could not believe it. So he went to the address at the back of the leaflet, to challenge them about it, which eventually led him to the person who gave it to him. He was invited to stay for dinner.

There he was, at a dining table, eating and listening to a couple about finding God. Convinced that the Lord Jesus is the way of salvation, he knelt down by the dining table and confessed his sins to the Lord Jesus Christ and invited Him to be his Lord and God. Billy said, "When I stood up, I felt that all my sins went out through my legs." His is the only story I have heard hundreds of times in the open air, and I never got tired of it. And he was very humorous too as he shared it. He was an entertaining speaker.

Unexpected Hospitality. Our team was led by Mike Wakely, a tall, 26 year old Englishman. We were in a small town, Bilgram, in the state of Uttar Pradesh (UP.) The OM truck of which Mike was the owner and driver, stopped right in the middle of a large bazaar, and we started to sing, preach the gospel and announce the special offer of the Gospel literature we had brought. There were two Gospels, three booklets and a Gospel tract with an invitation to a correspondence course on the life of the Lord Jesus in a plastic bag. They were sold for the price of a cup of tea. Many gathered to hear us, most of them out of curiosity. We usually sold many sets of the literature as they were affordable for all.

An older man, short and skinny, gladly heard us talk about the Lord Jesus Christ. Eventually he came near and invited us for lunch at his home. Looking at him, we could tell that he could not afford to provide lunch for our team of six young people. However, he insisted we have lunch with him and he would not accept any excuse from us. So we agreed to accept his hospitality.

After our morning outreach was done, by about 12.30pm, he came to call us to his home. It was a one-room mud hut in the slum of the town. He was a day labourer. What deeply moved us was that he had killed the only chicken he had so that we could have chicken curry with the rice and roti, which is the local unleavened flat bread, made of wholemeal wheat. Many years later, Mike Wakely wrote a book entitled 'Generosity' and he devoted two pages to this dear man as an example of "generosity, overflowing from a very big heart".

During the lunch, we found out he was the only Christian (Roman Catholic) in the town, and also over an area that stretched for many miles. U.P at that time had the lowest percentage of Christians in India (0.01%), a tiny minority, and most of them lived in cities like Jhansi, Lucknow or Allahabad. Many who professed to be Christians went back to Hinduism.

Another reason why I remember that incident very clearly was the joy of seeing another "Christian" as there were very few Christians in U.P. I used to question whether anyone outside my denomination was a real Christian. But here I was, so overjoyed to meet a person who called himself Christian. I forgot all about the huge differences between our faiths. God was using an extreme situation to teach me something important.

Our team was interdenominational. Mike was an Anglican, another team member was Baptist, and the others were from other groups or did not belong to any church at all as they had joined the team soon after salvation from a Hindu or Muslim background. Any one who had a clear salvation testimony could join the OM teams. It dawned on me that there are born again, God-fearing Christians outside my denomination. A tree is known by its fruit. The issue is not which denomination the person comes from. I was becoming an inter-denominationalist.

Readers make leaders. George Verwer encouraged OMers to read, and a wide range of books was made available to us, especially books in English. As we travelled in the OM truck, going from one town to the next for preaching and distributing Christian literature, I spent much time in reading. "The Knowledge of the Holy" by A.W. Tozer, "Knowing God" by J.I. Packer and "Peace with God" by Billy Graham were among the hundreds of helpful books the Lord provided for me. Reading has been a huge blessing to me. Dave Hicks introduced me to the New American Standard Bible. George Miley, another great OM leader, was keen that we also read good secular books. Once he gave me a copy of the Biography of Moshe Dayan, a Defence Minister in Israel. Another helpful book was: "The Road Less Travelled."

Me, a leader? 1968 I had been under several excellent leaders and I was happy and contented. One day a few teams came together in Varanasi. George Miley told me that he wanted me to lead a team. I was shocked. Another old vehicle had arrived in India from the UK, adding to the fleet of about 40 OM trucks in India at that time. George wanted to take people from some of the larger teams to form another team of six people. All my reasons against my leading a team did not convince George. His answer was: "Just keep close to God so that He can tell you what to do, and you can call on Him when you need to." Looking back, that was the best 'leadership course' I ever had. Of course I have had good examples to follow. One good example is worth a hundred sermons. Many things in life are caught rather than taught.

I was the youngest in the team assigned to me. One of the team members was three times my age - the former boxing champion from the UK, Billy Jones. But he was a real gentleman, sold out for Christ. He was a great encouragement to me. Chris Begg from New Zealand (now with the Lord), an extremely gifted young man, was part of the team for a while. I think George Miley put him with me to make sure I did not crumble under pressure. After a short time with us, he was given a team to lead in Orissa. The other three in the small team of six were from India, and they were new to OM.

This was how I began leading my first team in Varanasi, U.P, a top Hindu pilgrimage centre in India. It was a good start for learning leadership ministry. I had to depend on God as George had advised me, and God never fails. I remember God waking me up in the mornings, before the team woke up, for my quiet times and planning. Once, stones were thrown at us, but none of the stones hit me or any of the others in the team. God had more work for us to do.

God's wonderful provisions. I had been leading a large team of 14 brothers in Katihar in Bihar. It was monsoon season and continuous rain made our ministry in the streets difficult. This also meant we were not selling many books and so we were often without any money. We felt we had stayed long enough in Katihar and decided to move to the nearby city of Purnea, about 30 km away. But we did not have any money for the diesel for the huge OM truck, the BMC, which stalled every few thousand meters because of an air leak in the fuel system. The old vehicle also had a faulty self starter. So we all had to get down in the monsoon rain on to the muddy roads and push the truck to get it started!

We set out by faith, trusting the Lord for the fuel needed for the 30 km journey. I selected a stack of evangelistic books, waited on the road, and stopped one of the many trucks passing by. I gave the stack of books to the driver and told him we need fuel from his truck's fuel tank to enable us to get to Purnea. The driver was kind, and he gave us sufficient fuel for the journey. Excitedly we continued the journey, with the truck stalling every now and then due to the air leak in the fuel system.

We were just a few thousand meters from our destination in Purnea when a buffalo calf crossed the path of the truck. The truck hit the animal and stalled. The British driver, John Miles, started to pump the air out of the system so that the team could get out and push-start the engine. Although it was raining, the whole village came out in force, the men with long sticks in their hands and the women were all crying. They demanded 300 rupees from us because we had hit the calf. That was a lot of money in those days. But we had no money with us!

Thankfully, a jeep came by and an important looking tall man stepped out. He told the villagers we only need to give 30 rupees, since the animal was OK. He made them agree to that sum and I was told to give them the money. But I did not have 30 Rs to give them. The man with the jeep said that if he were to leave, they would demand from us 300 Rs again. I then asked, if he would be willing to pay them first, and I would borrow 30 Rs from a Finish missionary lady living nearby to repay him. He agreed to do so. We then drove off to the missionary's house, where our team was to be based for the next few weeks.

The exact amount The elderly missionary lady came out when she heard the jeep and the truck entering her compound. The moment I got off the jeep, she said, "Before I forget" and started to walk back into her house. She soon returned with a money order, sent to us at this address by Nicholas Narjinari and his OM team. I was surprised as I had not yet told anyone about the move to Purnea.

The message on the Money Order form read: "We were praying for you and the Lord impressed on our hearts to send you 30 rupees." It was signed "Nicholas Narjinari". Thank you Lord, and thank you Nicholas. The money was sent five days before we were in need of the exact amount of 30 rupees. My team and I were in the school of "Getting to know God" through such experiences, which were coming upon us thick and fast.

Among wild animals I was leading another team in Palamu District, in the south-western corner of the same state of Bihar. Palamu is now part of the newly formed state of Jharkhand. Recalling the time in southern Bihar (Jharkhand) brings back fond memories. Good sales of books, especially Bibles and the many meetings in the churches and Christian and government schools were unforgettable. Many nominal Christians were coming to the Lord. There were also many village markets all around where literally thousands would come with their farm produce to buy and sell. This was a good place and an effective way to reach thousands of people for the Lord through open air preaching and the selling of the Gospel literature.

One day we set out from Ranchi in a truck loaded with Gospel literature and headed for the next base during our month long operation in Palamu District. The driver was an American young man Terry Jones. We used the daylight hours for preaching in the villages along the way. Our host in a small Christian village was expecting us to arrive by late evening. It was already dark and cloudy, and we had to go through a long stretch of jungles on mud road to get to our destination. The jungles were known to have pythons, bears and other wild animals.

As we were driving down a hill, we came to an unexpected river in the valley. Instead of a bridge on the road to link the two hills, the village folks had simply filled up the valley with mud, with stonewalls on either side to keep the mud in. The water in rainy times was expected to fill up the one side and then overflow over "the bridge" and continue to flow down the valley. Terry drove up close to the crossing and asked the co-driver to check up the "bridge". He looked at it in the beam light of the truck, walked all over it, and then signalled Terry to drive in and up the hill. I was with the team in the back cabin of the truck.

Well, when we were fully on the "bridge", the truck, laden with the team members and the tons of Gospel literature, sank into the mud, and was about to tip over on its right side into a pool of water. All of us managed to crawl out of the back of the truck onto the road in the jungle. There was nothing we could do to get us out of that ditch. We felt helpless. I just did not know what to do. Terry got out of the driver side and came over to me and hugged me and started to sob. We gathered together and prayed, and asked the Lord for safety in the jungle that night. We also asked the Lord to hold back the rain so that we could sleep in the open under the stars. That night, we slept in the "many stars hotel".

And we did sleep well. We spread our sleeping bags over any space we could find among the bushes. The Lord did hold back the rain. The water subsided. I got up and counted the team and none was missing. The Lord had protected us from all harm.

Out of the ditch We were awakened by a truck early in the morning. We were in their way. We were delighted they were able to help us get out of the river within a short time so that we could continue on our way up the hill. They had every thing needed to pull us out of the ditch - several workers, plenty of ropes and a few big logs. It was clear to us there was divine intervention. Not many trucks went by that jungle road. The Lord had sent them. He knew where we were, the predicament we were in, and the kind of help we needed. The Lord was teaching us to trust Him in all situations and every aspect of our lives.

My first driving licence I was with another team in Cooch-Bihar in the Duars, bordering Bhutan. Dave Hicks was with us as the driver of our huge truck. We had a large team. The ministry opportunities abounded, especially in the weekly markets all around the district. Most days there was more than one market we could go to. The Swedish missionary in whose compound we were staying suggested that we divide our large team into two. One team would go with Dave in his truck. He offered his jeep for the smaller team. We liked the idea but we had no driver.

I knew how to drive but had never applied for a licence. So Dave and I did some driving around in the jeep and then went to the RTO's office to apply for a learner's licence. They made an exception and I was allowed to take a test the third day. The officer tested my driving skills in different ways. It included driving him to a shop where he needed to buy something. I passed the test and was given a licence. We thanked them and gave the officer a stack of evangelistic books. That was how we were able to double our efforts by functioning as two teams during the day.

Eight boiled eggs each One morning in Cooch-bihar we got up as usual, did our quiet time and cleaning up, and then walked down the road as usual to the roadside chai-shop (simple restaurants) for breakfast, which usually consisted of puri and tea. We noticed the street was empty and we learned that it was a "bandh" (closure) again. All the shops were closed and there was no traffic. This meant that we would have no food for the day, as we ate out in cheap restaurants. It also meant that we would not be able to go out to do evangelism. Well, we walked back to the missionary's house and reported the "bandh". He offered all the eggs we needed for the day from his poultry farm. So we all had eight boiled eggs each that day - two for breakfast, three for lunch and three for dinner. It was better food value than what we normally ate.

A severe attack on my faith overruled by God It took place some time during the late 60s. I went through a period, possibly several months, of doubts about God and the Bible. I did not tell anyone. I was already leading OM teams and I continued going through all the ministry

Beyond the Natural

motions and spiritual disciplines. The ministry continued to bear fruit. But I was trying to figure out whether God really exists. Is the Bible truly the Word of God? I was depressed. My faith in God and the Bible was under attack. I remember being temporarily helped by a chapter heading of one of AW Tozer's books I picked up in dire need of wanting an answer. The heading was: "God is incomprehensible". This made sense to me although the battle was still raging.

I came very close to giving up my faith and the Bible. How my parents would feel if I were to give up my faith was very much on my mind. My mother was already with the Lord. I knew my father would be devastated if I denied the faith. He had paid a big price for becoming the first believer in the large extended family and was beaten up by his father. "Is there a better faith than the Roman Catholic faith?" he was asked. But he stood firm and eventually saw many in the family join either a Brethren or Pentecostal group, including his father who became a committed Brethren believer.

In my mind, it was not right to follow the Bible if I was not truly convinced about God's existence and the Bible being God's Word. It came through to me that before I put the Bible aside and give up my faith; I should examine the matter more carefully by reading the Bible once through. I started to read the Bible from Genesis. I thought it would be the last time I would do so.

What I experienced as I read through the Bible was not what I expected. Every page spoke powerfully to me. "Yes, this is God's book," I kept saying as I read along. "Only God could have known this" or "only God could have promised this", or something like that. What impressed me most was the character of God, which came shining through its pages. The God of the Scriptures is so vastly different from the gods of Indian religions.

The Lord was merciful. He must have taken a special interest in my reading through the Bible. My eyes were opened as never before. The God of the Bible is so different from anything else and any other being. I was convinced no man could have contrived the content of

42

the Scriptures and the being of God as revealed in the Scriptures. His way of salvation is unique. It is a free gift, and we need not work for it. It is provided for us through the death and resurrection of the Lord Jesus Christ, and faith is the means by which anyone can receive this gift of salvation. Surely no man could have come up with this way of salvation. It came through strongly to me that there are so many indications that the Bible is the Word of God.

I was blessed. I was excited. I became fully assured that the Bible is inspired by God, God's Word to the world. I could believe Him and every word in His book – and I mean every word. This experience was a major turning point in my life. Such an attack of doubt about God and His Word has never occurred again. I am deeply thankful to our gracious Lord for turning the terrible attack on my faith in Him and His Word into a very helpful experience for me that laid a strong foundation for my faith in Him and in the Scriptures.

Since then I have had the joy of reading through the whole Bible in short periods of time - once in a month, another time in two months, reading 20 pages a day. I recommend reading the Bible through in a short time. Try it and you will see a difference. It has been said that the whole Bible can be read in 85 hours. Most books of the Bible can be read in one sitting or two. Why not try it? Give God and His Word priority. There is no book like it. Teaching the Bible gives me great joy.

Deliverance by angels? It happened some time in early 1970. We were in North Bihar and our team of 14 had many opportunities to preach and distribute the Gospel literature in different weekly markets held in open fields which brought in people from dozens of villages all around. One day I decided to take three days off to fast and pray. I think N.J. Varughese was leading the team daily into evangelism, and John Miles drove the big OM truck, a seven tonner. It transported the large team and tons of Gospel literature, enabling us to be a mobile team.

By the afternoon of the third day, I had had enough of staying back and so I decided to go out with the team, although still fasting. We got off the main paved road, turned right and drove over a mud bank at the edge of the field, and then turned left into an open space where we could park the truck with the back of the truck facing the multitude of people in the market. We opened up the tail board of the truck to serve as our preaching platform and to stack and display books. The loud speaker was placed on the roof of the truck so it could be heard by hundreds of people. It is not unusual to have a few hundred people gather to hear the singing and preaching each time. As usual there were thousands of people buying and selling.

We were excited. It showed in our singing and preaching and selling the Gospel literature, especially our main set of books. Billy Graham's book: "How to Find God", which sold for 50 paisa, was bundled together with a packet of books with two Gospels and three booklets and a tract and these were given free with it. They were going like hot cakes. Every thirty or forty minutes, a new audience would gather, attracted by the singing, and we would go through the preaching and selling process.

Although all was going well and the people were friendly, I had an uneasy feeling in me right from the start that something was going to go wrong that day. Everything went well for a couple of hours or more. But about 15 minutes before we would have normally packed and left, a man in his thirties came to the truck. The sight of all the people buying Christian books made him angry and he began to stir up the people against us. He told them we were trying to bring back the British to India and make all of them Christians. He ordered them not to buy the books. After that we were unable to sell any more books. A few who bought the books returned them and wanted the money back, because they were afraid of him.

We immediately packed our things. Nine team members had returned from among the crowd and got in the back cabin of the truck and locked themselves in. The day's intake, which was quite a lot of money, was kept in book boxes. They began to pray fervently, just like the believers did when the apostle Peter was imprisoned, as recorded in Acts 12. John Miles, having ensured the truck was closed properly, got into the driver's seat and began to turn the truck around, with me guiding him from the back.

We lingered along for a few minutes, giving time for the three missing team members (Rashem Raj Poudel being one of them) to come back to the truck. They should be able to see the tall truck moving away slowly, and should be running to it. After a short while I decided that it was better to save the eleven (including John and I) and lose three rather than lose all fourteen team members. I climbed up the passenger side of the front cabin and locked the cabin from the inside, in the same way as John had done his side. John started to drive but discovered that they had blocked the way with a bullock-cart across "the road". Angry mobs caught up and came in front of the truck and started to throw huge, dried mud blocks at the windscreen (for lack of stones). Amazingly, the windscreen did not break and that made them even angrier and more determined.

Then the action shifted to the driver side. They tried to unwind the glass window, pushing it down and succeeded a little, enough to put their hands through the gap and slap John on his face. They finally managed to slip their hands in and opened the door from the inside and pulled John down into the ditch. I saw John sit there in the ditch, resigned to his fate, but they left him alone. I opened the door and came down. They pushed me around the vehicle to the back, and then pushed me into the ditch. They then positioned me against the wall of the ditch and began hitting me on the chest and stomach. My shirt was torn. Some stood at the top of the ditch hitting me on the head with their shoes and sandals.

Just then, a jeep pulled up, and in it were three tall, well built men, dressed in suits, unlike the people there. As soon as they stepped out of the jeep, the entire crowd dispersed - they actually ran away. The three men ordered the bullock-cart to be removed and told us to follow them in the truck on to the road. I told them about our three missing team members. They said: "Do not stop for them. If we were to leave you, the crowd will come back…" So they got in the jeep and reversed it to the paved road, and we followed them. Once they got on the main road, they drove off and our truck was not able to catch up with them to thank them. Since it was already dark, both the jeep and our truck had the head lights turned on.

I was deeply concerned for the three missing team members. Thank God, just a few hundred meters on, there stood the three brothers, waiting for us to pick them up. We learned that they too were mobbed in the market. A strong man came into the crowd and freed them and brought them to the edge of the market, showed them the direction they should walk and told them where to wait for the truck. Praise God, we were all together and safe. The trouble of the preceding 30 minutes or so did not dampen the joy we had of seeing thousands of people being reached with the good news. Oh what lessons we were learning about God and the way He undertakes for His servants.

Unexpected "break" from North India

1971. It was not what I wanted but God used it for good. "How to make friends and influence people" has never been, sadly, one of my strong points. Well, my leader and I were growing apart. I did not stop to think about it. There were plenty of ministries to keep me occupied. I cannot even remember what it was all about. It was a relationship problem.

I was very surprised when two top OM leaders flew into Ranchi to talk to me. They were Thomas Samuel from Bangalore and George Miley from Bombay. They spoke mostly with my leader. Then to me, only to advise me to take a break from the north and join a team in Tamil Nadu where OM had just started an OM team. They were two leaders I respected greatly; still do, and therefore I did not try to change their minds or even ask why. Lo and behold, I was on a train, headed for the southern state of Tamil Nadu where an OM team was.

It would be wrong to give the idea that I was a happy person. Deep inside, I was angry. It took the Lord some time to help me from this bondage. I remember a time sitting on a rock in the field to do my quiet time but I was very resentful. I picked up a stone to throw at my leader thousands of KM away. God dealt with me there as I read through the epistle of 1 John. He showed me that He loved him as much as He loved me. He died to save him. That was a turning point.

Ebenezer Sunderaj. The team in Tamil Nadu was led by Ebenezer

Sunderaj. Like A.G. Philip the leader in Kerala, Ebenezer was among the "Thomas Samuel's Ten Men" who were specifically prayed into OM India by Thomas Samuel, the All India OM Coordinator. All of them were lecturers, engineers or in some other good professions which they gave up in order to serve God with OM India. Brother Ebenezer was a lecturer in electrical engineering at the post graduate department of Madras University. When he joined OM, Thomas Samuel wrote telling me all about him, and that he was sending him to be on my team. We were together for about three months. Then he began to lead teams in U.P State, and subsequently took over the OM leadership of the State.

Ebenezer remained one of the main leaders in OM India for several years until he ventured out into other mission leadership ministries. He continues to exert a tremendous influence in India. His first book: "The Confusion called Conversion" written in the 1980s, when still with OM, became a book read by opinion makers and decision makers in Indian society. He saw that there was an enormous amount of ignorance, prejudice and negative opinion about Christians and their activities in India which resulted in many hate campaigns and attacks on Christians.

K. Rajendran, a college student, and a young believer from a Hindu background was on that team in Tamil Nadu. He was ready to learn and grow in the faith and ministry. He picked up guitar playing rather quickly in spite of my discouraging him about it. I thought this interest would stand in the way of his developing as a preacher and leader. I was wrong. Music helped him in his leadership and preaching ministries. He was a good open air preacher and also a very good and able leader, with a deep interest in developing people.

I tried to learn Tamil, his language, but Rajendran said with a smile I was "slaughtering his lovely language". I am glad to say that I can at least read Tamil, very slowly. Tamil is a sweet language and there are many lovely Christian songs in this language. India has 1600 languages and dialects. We Indians love our own languages and dialects. Very few are able to maintain rational objectivity on this issue. Many are willing to die for it, and many have. And there are about 6000 languages and dialects in the world!

I am glad that OM helps to fuse us all into one. We often have to work in a third language, which means learning it. When you know a language, you are likely to love it. I tell myself that the diversity of languages goes back to Babel (Genesis 11) and it is one of the vivid reminders of our rebellion against God. Should we allow differences in cultures and languages to be one more divisive factor among believers who are one in Christ? The challenge is for believers to manage this issue and manifest our unity in Christ as a testimony to the world and to the glory of God.

Rajendran did not know the circumstances for my being on the team and away from North India. He asked Ebenezer, "Why he is not leading a team?" I hope it was not for this reason that Ebenezer was away a lot from the team and I found myself leading the team. Among other things he was setting up an OM office to coordinate more teams to work in Tamil Nadu. He did show up whenever there was a major crisis. One such crisis occurred when one of our team members drowned in a shallow river which had an uncovered pit – the hole was originally dug for a pillar for a huge bridge that was planned. We were so sad to learn from the fire brigade that others have died there before him.

The brother who died was an HBB from a Brahmin background. The last thing we did together as a team was a night of prayer, during which he prayed fervently with many tears for his parents, that they might come to know the Lord as their Saviour and God. On hearing the news of his death the parents came, and they stayed up all night, with the father thumbing through the son's Bible. They left the next morning, with their son's belongings, including his Bible. Would he have ever touched a Bible otherwise?

Rajendran served the Lord with OM Teams in North India for many years, including some time together with me, after I returned to Bihar. He also served in various leadership roles on the OM ship Logos, OM International and particularly in developing OM India training programmes in the 80s and early 90s. He married a young lady, Pramila, from U.P state. She is similarly gifted and together with her husband, is now serving in a high level mission leadership role in India and beyond. I had the privilege of speaking at their wedding.

Rajendran's book "Which Way Forward for Indian Missions?" is not only the result of extensive research but also the fruit of his first hand experience in reaching India with the good news. He has been in it for about 40 years and he has seen what we traditionally do with regards to missions in India. He sees a need for a change of paradigm in our doing missions if India is to be evangelised.

He is burdened to see the many Indian cities like Bombay and Kolkata, the 350 million middle class, the hundreds of millions of higher cast Hindus, the almost forgotten Muslim population of India and of course, all India, reached with the Gospel. Making this happen is like turning a huge ship around. It has to be done very slowly. It is beyond what the Indian church can do. Only God can bring it about. He is able. Let us be sensitive to what the Lord seeks to bring about and cooperate with Him.

His recent book "Heart to Heart" is a collection of his leadership letters that appeared in the editorial of the Indian Missions, the magazine of the India Missions Association of which he was the General secretary. IMA is one place where he has been able to stamp his leadership very deeply, having led it for over ten years. IMA is the largest missions association in the world. 200 of the 500 Indian missions, especially the bigger ones, are associated with IMA. God used him to see a tenfold growth during his leadership of the movement.

To the OM ship Logos for three months. One day, when I was still in Tamil Nadu, Ebenezer Sunderaj came to me with a passport application form, mostly filled up. OM India leadership had selected me among a dozen Indian OMers to join the newly acquired OM ship, the Logos. He was going to help me get my passport. All I had to do was sign the form and answer a few questions for him to fill the form with his good handwriting.

God's ship and God's men for God's work Shortly afterwards a few of us Indians boarded the ship in Madras (Chennai), joining George Verwer, the Director of the ship, Captain Bjorn Kristiansen from Norway, among 114 Christian staff and crew from many western nations. Our first port of call was Singapore, then Surabaya in Indonesia. We did not know it then, but it was the beginning of the vast expansion of OM ministry, from a handful of countries to a hundred nations. The OM ships, Logos, the Doulos, the Logos II and now the Logos Hope are well known today around the world.

George Verwer (USA) developed a vision of an ocean going ship for the ministry the Lord had given OM. His voyage to Europe on the QE II may have been used of the Lord to sow the seed in his mind. He had pages and pages written on how a ship can be used for world missions. Some of it read like science fiction, I am told, but it was really God's strategy - and just about everything in those pages became a reality. The ship materialised in answer to six years of prayer by many prayer partners in different parts of the world.

George Verwer was ably assisted by George Miley (USA), who had his start in OM as George Verwer's secretary. He had been George Verwer's right hand man in India for four years. George Miley was handpicked to lead, establish and develop further the Logos ship ministry, which he did for over the next 15 years. This included adding a much bigger ship, the M/V Doulos, to the OM Ships ministries.

How the composition of the crew came about was equally remarkable. Each one of the 43 crew members of the Logos had come to faith in Christ during the 6 years of prayer for the ship and its crew. Rashad Babukhan was a Muslim by birth but turned to God when he heard the Lord Jesus. He became our third officer. The Captain was a former communist, an atheist, an alcoholic. He dramatically recovered from a coma after heart surgery, and became a Christian. He heard about the OM ship vision and joined the movement even though we still did not have a ship. When the number of crew members we needed to sail the ship was complete, a few weeks later OM owned the Logos. Most of the money for buying the ship came in answer to prayer. What was taking place was breathtaking. It was a big boost to my own faith.

My first ever voyage. We left Madras on July 2nd 1971 at about 10.30 pm, sailing into pitch darkness. Everything was new to me. I had no previous sailing experience at all – not even on a dingy boat. The first few minutes sailing from the berth to the mouth of the harbour felt wonderful. But soon it changed - as we entered the open sea, our little ocean-going vessel of 2319 tons, 82 meters long, 13.44 meters wide and 5.5 meters underwater, was bobbing up and down like an empty bottle in a stormy sea. I was scared. I dared not stand around at the rail. I quickly ran down to my cabin and settled down on my bed. The shared cabin allocated to me was at the back end of the little ship. I had the lower bunk bed. Being at the back end of the ship was only a little better for sailing than being at the front end.

There I was, holding on to the bed, very sure that we would all sink with the ship. Our gracious Lord knew how I felt, and He tenderly spoke to me: "He who upholds all things by the word of His power". I knew that it was from Hebrews chapter 1 of the King James Bible. I knew God would uphold the ship and I would be alive in the morning. I slept well. The sea was calmer when I woke up in the morning. I walked up onto the deck, with the tropical sun brightly shining down on us. All I could see was sea, sea, and more sea - not even an island anywhere. We were probably less than two hundred miles from Madras.

It took us about six days to get to Singapore. We were living on German bread, meat, potatoes and boiled vegetables, prepared by our amazing German cook (now with the Lord) and his European assistants. This was a huge shock to my taste buds, and a shock to my system - probably in the head but very real. I had only recently added the north Indian chapatti and daal to my diet. How we wished we had brought some pickles with us. This was the beginning of my eating a huge variety of food from around the globe. Now they all taste wonderful, and I am no longer hung up on hot curry and rice. But it took time to adjust. What an amazing variety of food is out there.

All of us were on a steep learning curve. Less than a third of us were longer term OMers. The rest were new OMers or straight from the shipping world, who knew about ships but did not have experience in the ministry, and we had to learn to work together. We needed one another. It was not easy for most of us. I had a lot to learn, especially learning to appreciate and respect the ministry men and women who serve God with their professions, and seeing them as equal to those who are engaged in the ministry of the Word. The body of Christ is made up of different members who contribute in different ways. Christians who serve God with their own hands and finance cannot be over esteemed.

Singapore. We were in Singapore from July 8 to August 10, 1971. In those days, the ship used to stay about a month in each port. God opened many doors for ministry in Singapore, especially to believers where we shared the OM story and OM vision, especially highlighting some unreached countries like India and Nepal. Many churches and denominations welcomed us warmly. We even tried to do mass evangelism by going out onto the streets and distributing tracts specially printed for the Singapore visit. We distributed them in the thousands. However, most of the recipients of the tracts threw them away and littered the streets. This was in spite of the strict laws in Singapore against littering. I don't think we distributed tracts in that manner again in Singapore. What was a suitable method for India was not suitable for all countries.

Surabaya, Indonesia. After a short voyage we reached Surabaya, Indonesia for a month long programme, from August 14 till September 14, 1971. We arrived at the tail end of the great Revival that swept Indonesia for many years, which brought many to the Lord, including large numbers of Muslims. We heard of the many miracles that took place during that period. The churches were large and thriving. They were very good at singing. It is clear to me that good singing is a blessing of the Holy Spirit to aid us in our worship, evangelism and discipleship.

Large numbers of people visited the ship in Surabaya to see the book display or to attend one of the many meetings on board. Christian films projected against the side of the ship in the evenings were watched by hundreds of people. Many churches opened their pulpits for us to minister. Hundreds indicated they wanted to follow the Lord. One of my vivid memories is being on a team going inland with George Verwer, visiting a Bible School and churches. I was George's co-driver. Most of the team members were from India, and had been with OM India for several years. We got to see George up close. We were amazed at his diligence in making good use of his time. When I was driving, he would be dictating letters from the back of the van. Good stewardship of time is one of the many things OM imparted to us. We would often hear George say, "Redeem the time."

It was easier for us to minister and relate to the people in Singapore because most Singaporeans understood English. However, it was a joy to relate with the Indonesians because of their charming ways and their love for singing. They can sing well and they are able to form a choir with total strangers in no time. I think singing and church-growth goes together. A happy faith is very attractive. The grace of the Lord sets our heart free in joyful singing unto the Lord, in worship of Him. It is interesting to note that Christianity is the only religion that expresses worship of God in songs. The Scriptures exhort us to sing, many times. All heaven sings in worship of God. And we have someone to sing about.

What we were able to accomplish in these ports demonstrates the great potential of a ship for world evangelism, discipleship and mobilising Christians into missions. The ship was also a great tool to impart mission visions to these countries which were primarily seen as mission fields. I shall remember these ports as the first ports to give the ship ministry a very warm welcome - from believers, the press and also from the crowds that visited the ship daily, buying large quantities of Christian and educational books. There were also various kinds of programmes on board for believers and the non-Christian public. We made many friends. It was painful to sail away, leaving these dear people behind. God had great things in store for the OM Ship ministries.

The ship people were highly motivated, and ready to make adjustments according to the situations that arose. We ate all around the ship while our dining room was used for meetings, including a three day pastors' conference. Some of the ship leaders preached four times on a Sunday at meetings on shore. They would usually take a team from the ship to give singing items, testimonies etc. There were meetings on board every day. There were no off days as there was a sense of urgency.

Although we were an international community, most of the ship crew and staff were Caucasians at this stage. The rough looking deck crew, each one with a knife tied to his side, apparently needed for the job, would be rushing about. I was not used to Christians shouting and yelling at one another. I was scared. I felt more comfortable with the seasoned OMers, most of them Americans and British. There was a friendly Mexican family and also a warm Brazilian family on board. All of us had a lot to learn. It took us some time to learn to adjust to one another but we did learn to work together. I was like a horse with its blinkers on. I wanted to get back to North India as quickly as possible. It was not easy for me to change but God graciously worked in my heart, often gently and imperceptibly.

Back to Bihar. A letter came from Chris Begg, a British OMer serving in Bihar. He was on my first team in Varanasi, U.P. He was leading teams in Bihar at this time and he wrote, giving reasons why I should return to Bihar. It seemed right to me. That was where the need was greatest. India was wide open for the Gospel and it would be good to make the most of the open doors. At that time, I thought North India was God's call for my life ministry. When the ship returned to Cochin, India, on the 6th of October after a 12 day dry dock in Singapore, I left the Logos and headed for Bihar.

Resham Raj Poudel I went back to my former role of team leader with a team of people from all over India and one or two from abroad. One of my team members was Resham Raj Poudel, a former Brahmin priest from Nepal. He suffered much for the Lord in Nepal, including being tortured during imprisonments. He was sent to India to avoid further imprisonment, at the advice of some church leaders in Nepal. We served together for nearly three years. I can still see him with a big stack of Gospel literature, limping up and down the streets, witnessing to the people. He limped because the police in Nepal had dislocated his knee to stop him from continuing with his preaching.

Nepal was a mountainous region and often one has to go on foot. Resham has since returned to Nepal, planting hundreds of churches and leading thousands of Nepalese to the Lord, mostly on foot. He and his wife Sita founded Nepal Gospel Centre, an evangelistic movement with a strong discipleship emphasis. It is amazing what is going on in Nepal these days. The believers there have found an effective strategy for the evangelisation of Nepal as well as for the Nepalese outside Nepal.

Mysteries I do not understand Another key team member was Samson Nayagam from Tamil Nadu. There had been a huge turn around in his life after he committed himself to the Lord. I met one of his cousins many years later in England and they could not believe that he was saved and was serving the Lord. I only knew the new Samson, although he had told me a few things of his past life. He was a born leader and he led OM teams for several years in North India. Later he married Premlata, a great young lady from south Bihar and they served the Lord together. But sadly, within a few years of their marriage and the birth of their daughter, Samson was killed in a tragic bus accident.

Why would the Lord take such people to himself when they are so much needed here on earth? I must confess I do not understand why God takes away key people in the prime of their lives and service - like Stephen in the Bible, and several of my friends over the years. Chris Begg, who was on my first team also died in a tragic vehicle accident together with his Swedish wife and two Americans travelling with them. He was an Oxford graduate, gifted in so many ways, including music and a special talent for putting the Scriptures to music. We still sing some of his choruses. One of them is Habakkuk 2:14 put to music: "For the earth shall be filled with the knowledge of the glory of the Lord as the waters cover the sea". We know that "all His (God's) ways are just" and "He does all things well". I know that He knows best. In any case He is worthy of all we can offer Him, even our very lives.

Leadership Training. The year 1973 started off really well for me. I led the biggest team of 14 men with the biggest OM truck in India. It was loaded with tons of Christian literature, mostly Gospels portions that we sold in sets of two Gospels and three booklets put together in a plastic bag. We enjoyed good fellowship and team work. I was 23 years old. Ron Penny about 35 years old, a British OMer, was the Regional Leader, overseeing the work of OM in four states: U.P, Bihar, Bengal and Orissa. He oversaw several teams in the region.

"Lord, what am I to do with this team of 14?" I asked the Lord. "Leadership training" was what I sensed the Lord would have me do. I concentrated on training three of the 14 young men to prepare them for team leadership. I believe the Lord taught me how to go about it. The three men were C.K. Thomas (now with the Lord), Pran Ranjan Paricha and K.Rajendran. They came from three different Indian States; Kerala, Orissa and Tamil Nadu.

As far as I was aware, the only book available on Christian Leadership in India was one with that title written by A.E. Norrish. "Spiritual Leadership" by Oswald Sanders was not available then. Subsequently there has been an abundance of leadership titles. We studied the book section by section daily, for an hour. We then sought to understand the subject of leadership from some of the Bible characters. It is amazing the wide variety of subjects the Bible covers. It touches every aspect of our lives, ancient or modern. It is a manual for living, not just how to get out of hell.

When we went out for daily evangelism, I divided the whole team into three groups, with the three brothers leading one group each. In those days, the emphasis was on practical training and learning by doing. We wanted people who could do the job and not merely those able to talk. I did become a little nervous towards the end, wondering what the next step would be. What should I do with the three men who were all able to lead a team each? To my surprise and joy, when I returned with the team to our base, now in Ranchi (South Bihar/Jharkhand), Ron Penny informed me that there had been an increase of new recruits and he needed two new team leaders. C.K. Thomas and Pran Ranjan were chosen. They proved to be good team leaders.

I was still one of the team leaders. Rajendran remained on my team together with a few of the others like Resham Raj from Nepal. I made Rajendran the acting leader of the team. I remember the many hours Rajendran and I spent together, praying for team matters and the evangelisation of India, especially when travelling together on the back of rickshaws. Shortly after that, Rajendran was also asked to lead a team. Eventually, Resham Raj and other team members were given team leadership responsibilities too. I learned that God does not waste manpower. There is a prepared place for every prepared man. Do you have a message to preach? God has a place for you to preach it.

Years later, Rajendran, who was from a Hindu background, told me that one of the great contributions of OM India was the nurturing of Hindu converts on the teams. Although OM India had a rule that all who join OM must have at least a year of church affiliation, many HBBs and MBBs were allowed to join the team right away. I know one OMer who joined the team the day after he received the Lord. He had been witnessed to by an OMer on the streets of Delhi. Today he is a key Christian leader serving the people of Orissa.

I met a former OMer after several decades. He had served in another part of India. He was one of those who joined OM India shortly after his conversion because of persecution from his parents and his community. Subsequently, his relationship with his family was restored and he led 300 of his Hindu village people to the Lord. Almost half of them were his relatives. His parents opened their home for believers to meet for Sunday worship. He urged me to tell Hindu converts to try their best not to sever their family relationships. "Who else will evangelise them?" he asked.

North India is not all the World

I was taken by surprise but on looking back, I see God had orchestrated it, even using my failures. God was on course even though I was not. He wanted me on the Logos for a longer term. However, no Indian OMer was allowed to be on the ship more than a few months in those days. It was amazing to me that here I was in Ranchi (near Calcutta) one evening, having absolutely no thoughts of leaving North India and on the third day , I was standing on board the Logos, in Bangladesh, about to sail to Singapore. I arrived two hours before the ship's scheduled departure time.

It was remarkable how it all turned out. My passport was in the OM head office in Bombay, on the west coast of India. I also needed to get a visa for Bangladesh before I could leave India or get into Bangladesh. Wow, what God is able to do! And He did not give me any prior indication. I was oblivious to what was about to take place. Perhaps the Lord did try to let me know but I was stone deaf, or He knew it would be a waste of time to tell me as I had made up my mind to be in Bihar for the rest of my life. In any case, I want to say, thank you Lord! His ways are indeed higher and better than my ways, and our ways are not His ways (Isaiah 55:8-9). This is how it worked out.

The evening of May 30th 1973. It was about 5.30 pm, judging from the twilight outside. I fell out with my leader towards the end of a leadership meeting of about ten people. There was plenty of ignorance and pride in both of us. I felt there was a little bit of the colonialist superiority complex mentality on his part which I resented. It became clear one of us had to leave. The solution was obvious. I offered to leave, with no idea of what I would do next. I was promptly given a hundred rupees, enough money for me to return home to Kerala - a three days train journey in those days.

Painful goodbye. We ate supper together and I said goodbye to the brethren, most of whom were my team members, either then or in the past. Having to say goodbye to them under such circumstances was more painful to me than my being jobless or the humiliation I felt. I was driven in an OM vehicle to the train station in Ranchi to catch the train to Calcutta, then another to Madras, and finally a third train to Kottayam, Kerala. The deep darkness outside reflected how I felt on the inside.

Divine arrangement At the ticket counter, I felt I should not buy a ticket all the way to Kerala, but only up to Calcutta (Kolkata today), for two reasons. I must stop there and tell my story to Dave Hicks, the OM leader based there. I also wanted to reserve a sleeping berth rather than sit, possibly even stand, for three days all the way to Kerala. I arrived at the team base in Calcutta at about 3.00 pm. The first man I met as I walked into the OM house in Calcutta was George Miley, the Director of Logos. This was totally unexpected as he and his wife Hanna were in the USA on home leave, and after that they were to return to the Logos in Chittagong, Bangladesh.

They were on their way back to the ship in Chittagong, via Bombay and Calcutta and they had decided to visit their former co-workers. George Miley who ministered for several years in India with OM till he was appointed Director of the ship ministry had been my leader for some years during that period. Hanna also worked in Bombay, and knew many ladies there. Hanna needed one more day in Bombay whereas George needed a day in Calcutta. So George left Hanna in Bombay and went on ahead of her to Calcutta, with the plan to meet up the next day at Calcutta airport and leave together for Chittagong.

George had arrived at the OM base in Calcutta three hours before me, and had telephoned Ranchi to find out how things were there. He already knew what happened to me and had been wondering how to contact me. As I walked in, he asked, "What do you plan to do now?" I replied, "Well, go home and think things over and see what the Lord wants next." He said, "Don't go home. Come with me to the Logos." I thought to myself, "George, yes. Logos, no." But then, I had nowhere else to go.

I agreed. And a dark cloud cleared from my head. I told George that my passport was not with me but in the Bombay OM office. He said, "Hanna is in Bombay now and she is flying in tomorrow morning. She can bring the passport." So George Miley called the Bombay office and told Alfy Franks to release my passport and hand it to Hanna. He must have called a few other offices, perhaps including George Verwer, as what was being done was a big exception to the rule. He was able to carry it through because of the relationships he had cultivated and the services he had rendered in OM since 1966. He was regarded in those days as the number 2 in OM after George Verwer.

I did not manage to narrate my part of the story to Dave Hicks as I had intended. Next morning George and I went to the airport to meet Hanna. The three of us rushed to the Bangladesh Embassy, got my visa, went back to the airport and then on to the ship in Chittagong. George had contacted the ship too, so that my name was added to the immigration and customs list of people sailing with the ship and also on the list of people arriving in the next port. There was also a cabin for me.

The Lord had in his sovereign power and wisdom undertaken for all that had taken place, to hew me out of India and plant me on the Logos, and thereafter on two other OM ships, for a total of 15 years. Subsequent attempts on my part to get back to India backfired in my face, including one which stretched out for three years, for which my family paid a high price. It is not wise to be stuck with your own mission plans and not stay open to the Lord for Him to lead.

God heals I came on the ship, a very deeply wounded man. The two key people God used to heal me and chart my life in the 70s were George Miley and Frank Dietz. The way they accepted me in words and actions, and the opening up of ministry opportunities, all contributed to the healing process. There is a crying need for such men and women in the body of Christ. I would like to be like them.

I learned later that George and Frank, who were Director and Assistant Director of the Logos respectively, had been praying about getting me to assist them with the training programmes on the Logos. I became involved in ministry in the many Asian countries the ship visited, as much as I was ministering on board the ship.

I reported to Frank, who had the huge responsibility of the day to day running of the ship ministry. He was responsible for the personnel, programme and training departments as well as accommodation and finance - just about everything on the ship. He was also the main speaker on the Logos. His office was a cupboard transformed into an office. Space was at a premium on the little Logos. Initially only 114 people could travel on the ship, but the number was increased later when accommodation including a dormitory was added at the front of the ship.

George Miley had oversight of the ship ministry. He concentrated on the ship's ministry in future ports and those who went ahead to line up the port programmes. He liaised with the OM offices which provided vital support in mobilising prayer, finance and new recruits to replace those constantly leaving after their short term commitments. The captain and the department heads such as the chief engineer and the chief officer were responsible to him. He preached more to the ship company than to those who came on board the ship for the various conferences and seminars. I still carry around with me the duplicated notes of about 30 studies he did with us on the doctrine of God. Oh, how we need a clear understanding of what the Bible teaches us about God. George's main contribution was leadership development of people on board.

It was no small job to pioneer the ship ministry. Never had so many professional seamen and ministry people worked together in such a confined space. It was an explosive situation. Both the directors had plenty on their plates but they were good at delegating responsibilities. George Miley once told me, "Never do something that someone else can do and learn in the process." One day George called me to his office. He said, "Chacko, there are some things that only you can do. There are some things only I can do. There are some things we both can do." I stood there wondering where this talk was going.

Well, he wanted me to take a meeting on shore which was scheduled for him. He had some important matters to attend to, without which the ship's departure for the next port would be delayed. It had something to do with the finance for refuelling of the ship. We had a hand to mouth existence in those days. I only had enough time to take a shower, change and leave for the meeting, at the same time prayerfully looking to the Lord for what He wanted me to preach at this meeting. This was in Indonesia and the meeting was in a Bible College. I preached on Prayer, highlighting prayer points the Bible gives. For example to pray to the Lord of the harvest to send out workers (Matt 9:37-38) and pray for open doors for the Word (Col. 4:3). This was the beginning of my five years with the Logos.

Little is much when God is in it. It was June 1973 and the ship was berthed in Jakarta, the capital city of Indonesia. This was the period when many were turning to the Lord in this country. A programme for the Christians of Bandung had been organised and Frank Dietz, one of the ship leaders would be there to speak in the main meetings. I led a small support team up to Bandung in a VW van driven by Morris John, loaded with books and Gospel tracts.

On the way to Bandung, we drove past villages with shops on either side of the road and many people milling about the streets, and we did what we would have done in India. A small bunch of tracts was flexed so that it loosened up, and then we threw it up as high as we could into the air from a fairly fast moving van. This usually resulted in the tracts floating up in the air, and then when they floated down, the people would run to catch them or pick them up from the road. We did exercise care to ensure lives were not endangered by the presence of other vehicles.

During the week of ministry in Bandung, a Christian leader had wonderful news for us. He told Frank Dietz that in a particular village, 23 people who picked up the tracts we had thrown along the way had a dream that night from God. They were told in the dream to go to a particular headmaster in the area and ask him to explain to them the meaning of the leaflet, otherwise they would perish. All 23 did as they were instructed in the dream, arriving at the headmaster's door in the early morning. He shared with them the Gospel and led them to receive the Lord Jesus Christ as their Saviour and Lord! And the church there was preparing them for baptism. I look forward to meeting all of them in heaven.

Sudan, Africa. In October 1973, the Logos sailed to Sudan. We had a programme in the port city, Port Sudan. The capital, Khartoum was inland, an overnight journey from the port city. A huge programme was organised for Khartoum, including a large exhibition of books. Ken Bullier, a tall deck officer from England and I were selected to go as guards for the railway carriage filled with educational and Christian books. It was an open carriage and we both sat on top of the books which were covered by canvas. Most of the journey was through the desert at night. And when we arrived at our destination, the people who came to collect the books could not tell the difference between the two of us - both of us were covered in dust and looked about the same colour. The books were off loaded and we had a good programme there in Khartoum.

The team members stayed with different Christian families. I stayed in the home of an Indian family, Dr. and Mrs M.M Ninan. He was a lecturer in the university. They made my stay so pleasant that Sudan became one of my favourite countries, although it was desert land. I learnt that it is the people who make you love a country. I have been blessed with other friends from this country.

George Miley decided to go inland, to minister in the city of Juba in South Sudan. I was in the two man team. On the plane I learnt that I was to be one of the conference speakers. When I said I did not have any conference messages, George passed me his ring notebook of sermon outlines and asked me to select sermons from it. A young British couple, David and Ann Fieldsend were attending the conference and they became my first ever financial supporters. They have been supporting me all these years. They are one of two couples who support me financially even though they are in the ministry themselves.

Kamal Fahmi George Miley wanted Sudanese representatives on the ship. We managed to recruit our first Sudanese, Kamal Fahmi, a 17-year-old youth, the son of the director of the Bible Society in Khartoum. His main qualification besides being a believer was that he spoke English. As he was not near a major OM recruiting area like Europe, USA or India, for his OM orientation he became my cabin mate. I supervised his listening to the OM orientation tapes and the reading of the set of books which were OM required reading.

Kamal served in the Book Exhibition department. In his Arab clothes, he was quite an attraction in the ports we visited, especially in the Far East. He became well-known for welcoming each one of the thousands of people who came on board with loud words of welcome and low bowing. I wondered whether he suffered from any back problems as a result of all that bowing – but perhaps his back became stronger for it. He did well on Logos. Finally he went back to Sudan and started the OM work in Sudan.

One of the yearly projects he had in his country was called "Floating Holy Bible Exhibition" which was held on a hired ship on the Nile River. Here is what Kamal said about it: "During my time on the ship Logos, God put in my heart to start something similar to OM India in Sudan. I returned to Sudan from the ship in 1975 after spending some time in Turkey. We started OM Sudan in 1976. We were involved in church mobilization, evangelism through literature distribution, film shows and summer outreach.

65

"One of the things we started in Sudan which we found very effective in reaching Muslims was Christian book exhibitions. We had many opportunities to talk to people and answer their questions, explain more about the Gospel and introduce them to a wide variety of Christian books. We could also show them films. People could sit in a coffee-bar setting in a friendly atmosphere and talk about the Gospel. We held the first book exhibition in the Khartoum University Campus in 1976. Subsequently we had it in the same venue where the Logos had its book exhibition in 1973. Christian books were displayed and sold publicly.

"In 1980, the exhibition hall we used in the centre of Khartoum was burned down because of an accidental fire. Without a suitable place for Christian book exhibitions, God put in our hearts to use a steamer instead. We rented a steamer from the Nile transport company owned by the government. One deck was used for the book exhibition and another deck for the various programs. We served food and drinks and showed Christian films in the evenings, and in the afternoons we had Nile cruises with Christian programs.

"The Minister of Information was always invited to open the exhibition and most of the time he came personally. Sometimes he was represented by his undersecretary. In 1983, President Numeri, the president of the country paid an unexpected visit to the exhibition. It was the same year he implemented Islamic law in Sudan. He received a copy of the Bible and kissed it.

It was an incredible way to share the Gospel in a friendly atmosphere and for families to have a nice Nile cruise while at the same time being exposed to the Gospel message and Christian literature.

"About 15,000 people would visit the exhibition in 2 weeks. It was advertised in the newspapers, on television and through pamphlets and posters. It brought the Gospel to the market place. It made it natural for Muslims to have Christian books and for Christians to share their faith publicly, not only in Khartoum but all over the country, as we held the Floating Holy Bible Exhibition for 17 consecutive years. The

Gospel was shared with many and God's word went into many homes. Many workers were raised and trained to serve the Lord.

"It gave an opportunity for all members of the body of Christ to be involved in ministry and be trained to share their faith. About 100 participants were involved in selling tickets, crowd control, cooking, selling and serving food and drinks, carrying boxes, cleaning, driving, shopping, singing, playing instruments, acting, teaching, preaching and sharing the Gospel. We had devotions every morning and a time of prayer. The evening ended with a time of prayer and sharing. It was a great time of training and discipleship."

The OM work eventually spread to other areas of North Africa and Kamal has become the leader for the Middle East and North Africa region, which includes most of the Muslim countries west of Pakistan. Kamal obviously is a visionary as well as bold for the Lord. God needs such people in hard places to serve Him. I reproduced his email because it gives you an idea of how a ship can be used in Christian mission.

Ethiopia The Logos ship then visited Massawa, Ethiopia (22 Oct-15 Nov). A large team including the ship choir, the Logos Singers, went inland to Addis Ababa and held a huge book exhibition as well as having programmes in the churches. I was not selected for this team. The book exhibition in the city was opened by Emperor Haile Selassie, who claimed to be a descendant of King Solomon.

I had more than enough I was on the smaller team in Asmara, with a similar programme. TV Varughese (from Kerala, India) was the team finance man and he was also in charge of the book exhibition we held in the city. There were a few days I could take off for a time of fasting and prayer. I had decided to eat at about 3pm on the third day. I needed money from Varughese to buy food from a street side restaurant. Varughese as usual went with the team to the book exhibition in town, assuring me that he would be back by 2pm. But by 3pm Varughese was still nowhere to be seen. Just then an Eritrean young man came by, one of the several friends we had made while ministering there. He said he was going to a restaurant and invited me to join him for a snack. So in a little hut-like teashop, we had a bread roll and a glass of milk each.

We then made our way back to the hostel where the team was staying. There were two girls waiting for me, whose mother had sent for me to join them for tea. So I followed these girls to their nearby home. Besides having tea, there was a small table spread with different kinds of cookies and cakes. I was well fed by now. Again I was back at the hostel, and two young people from the hostel said, "We looked everywhere for you." Well, the mother of these two students had sent some home-cooked food for them and they wanted to share it with me. So I went to their room and had a good meal with them. Believe me I was very full by then. Varughese, who came back very late that night, had forgotten all about me but God did not. I had more than enough.

We left Ethiopia and made a short stop in Djibouti for fuel, and then for a week of ministry in Dubai. In those days we had to do low-key-evangelism in Middle Eastern countries. In subsequent years, the doors were opened wider, enabling us to stay for longer periods of time for greater ministries. After a stop in Saudi Arabia, again for fuel, the ship sailed for India, our destination Bhavnagar, Gujarat. George Verwer joined the ship for this voyage. Being on the ship was one way he could visit India and minister to the OM teams in the country, besides ministering to the ship people. George is well-known as a speaker and a leader in world missions, but many of us in OM also deeply appreciate his pastoral ministry.

Em Namuco While we were yet at sea, Frank Dietz, the assistant director of the Logos called Em Namuco to his office. Em, a good friend of mine, is from the Philippines and was very active with the Logos Singers, although his duty on the ship was in the galley (kitchen). While in Ethiopia, Em came down with a bad case of dysentery and he had to be always near a toilet. The ship's doctor and nurse had been treating him but with little success. The ship people had been given instructions on how to look after their health when visiting different countries. But Em thought to himself, "I have been a missionary among head hunters in the Philippines and have eaten anything and everything, so the rule does not apply to me." Well, it did.

Frank wanted Em Namuco to join the OM India teams in Orissa during the five months the ship visited various ports around India and Sri Lanka (Bhavnagar, Bombay, Colombo, Galle, Pondicherry, Paradeep and Visakhapatnam). The idea was to give Em maximum exposure to OM work in India before his one year commitment with the ship ended and he would return to his home country. But Em protested, saying that he was suffering from dysentery and needing to be always near a toilet. Frank replied, "Never mind Em, you get sick in India anyway, before or after, it doesn't matter." Em said a quick prayer to the Lord and gave in to the decision to go.

One evening, about half way through the port visit, Em came down the gangway all packed and ready to head for Orissa, via Bombay by train. He had never been to India. At the bottom of the gangway, unknown to Em, were a few people loading the van and ready to go to the OM office in Bombay. There was one space left. Em was glad to take it and have company all the way to Bombay. He settled himself down in the van, thinking he would need many toilet stops along the route. To his surprise, he did not need any at all till the van reached the OM base in Bombay. He was healed and enjoyed his five months in Orissa and Bengal with plenty of ministry opportunities. Em, who joined OM for a one year term, is still with OM, having given about 20 years to the OM ship's ministry.

The angel of the Lord encamps around those who fear Him, and rescues them. My practice whenever the ship was in India was to leave the ship to be with the OM India land teams and contribute whatever I could. On this occasion, I was with a team from the ship driving down in a VW van to Bombay, to the OM head Office. George Verwer was in the group as this gave him more time in Bombay, where he used to live and run the OM work. It was an overnight drive and George would not allow us to stop even for a cup of tea as he wanted to be in Bombay before the office traffic started.

We arrived very early in the morning at the outskirts of Bombay. It was very quiet and we had the whole road to ourselves. Soon we saw thousands of people standing on both sides of the street. George was driving and at the passenger door was Alfy Franks, the all India coordinator. I was in the middle in the front with them.

For about five minutes, a Bible verse kept coming to me. It was Psalm 34:7: "The angel of the Lord encamps around those who fear Him, and rescues them." I wondered why these words kept coming to me, and it was growing in intensity. I had never had such an experience before. I could not control it. Was I going mad? And then, stones struck our front windscreen, shattering it into hundreds of pieces and bending one of the metal bars. Thankfully none of us were hit. George immediately stopped the van and came out with his hands up as a gesture that we were peaceful people and not hostile.

At that moment, from among the thousands of people, a group of police officers surrounded us and our vehicle. At first I feared the situation was going from bad to worse. But as it turned out they protected us from the mob. We then realised it was a "bandh", a day of political strikes when no vehicle was supposed to be on the road for the whole day.

The police escorted us and the vehicle to the police station where we took shelter for the whole day. We had to go hungry that day, as no shops were open. Although disappointed, George as usual sprang up into "redeeming the time" and was busy interviewing some of us and dictating letters, catching up on his correspondence and prayer times. We all had some free time to get to know one another better. I think George appreciated some undisturbed hours with Alfy Franks, who was leading OM India at that time with Ray Eicher. We left the police station when traffic resumed in the evening. God and His angels had surrounded us and delivered us.

*Chacko Thomas in front of an OM Display
on board the MV Doulos in 1990.*

Chacko, Sheela, Sunil, and Radha in the Philippines in 1990.

Chacko and Radha

On OM Ship Logos to South East Asia

I rejoined the ship in Bombay and continued with her ministry in two ports in Sri Lanka (Colombo and Galle) and for the ports on the east coast of India - primarily Pondicherry and Paradeep, where Em Namuco rejoined the ship.

Safety. While the ship was in Colombo, I was part of a team that went to minister in Jaffna, at the north end of Sri Lanka. After the week long programme, a group of us left Jaffna, late in the evening, and I drove non stop all the way back to the ship in Colombo. We reached our destination at 2am. Driving on the unlit streets with only the headlights of the vehicles for light and sitting for many hours just looking straight ahead made my neck stiff. Yes, I should have stopped for breaks, according to the OM rules. There were times when I did not know where the road was, especially when we were taking sharp bends in pitch darkness. I knew it was the Lord who had kept us safe that night. I was glad to be alive with the team when we finally reached our destination – but the others in the vehicle were apparently unaware of the dangers we went through. Our safety, including when driving, comes from the Lord.

Penang. The Logos left the east coast of India from Port Vishakhapatnam, the fuel and food port, and headed for Penang in West Malaysia, a four day voyage. The team were busy whenever the ship was in port and these voyage times were helpful for them to be alone as a ship family and also to prepare for future ports. The deck and engine crew had plenty of repairs and maintenance to do in their respective departments. They were assisted by available hands in the ministry, programme and exhibition departments. The kitchen and accommodation crew had extra work like shampooing the carpets or maintaining the wooden floor which had been trampled on by thousands of people who attended the various programme events every day. It was a special treat if the sea was calm, especially for people like me who get seasick easily. With the constant turnover of crew and staff, it was a good time to get to know the shipmates.

We arrived in Penang on the 29th of April 1974 for ten days of ministry. It was good to see many Chinese, Malays and Indians come on board to benefit from the large display of books, and I guess the novelty of visiting a ship. During future visits, the Malays, who were mostly Muslims, were forbidden by the government to visit the ship because of the Christian books at the book exhibition, although up to 60-70 per cent of the books were educational, good for all. We had to have a board at the gangway saying "For non-Muslims only". It was also stated in the newspapers, TV and radio advertisements: "Non-Muslims only". This did not stop people from coming.

One of my jobs on the ship was to share prayer requests for India, Nepal, Pakistan and Bangladesh in the many conferences for believers, pastors and Christian leaders held on board the ship. It was amazing to see people crying out to God for the evangelisation of India and her neighbours. God used the ship all over the world to mobilise prayer for India and it gave me a special sense of doing something significant for India, although I was not there physically.

Singapore. The next port was Singapore where the ship made its 7th visit. Because of its strategic location, we had to go by Singapore on our way to the east or on our way back to India. Singapore may well be the most visited port in the world by the OM ships. We continued to present the world mission challenge, especially for the Hindu and Muslim world where millions have yet to hear the name of Jesus as

Lord and Saviour for the first time. Soon an OM office was opened here to facilitate recruiting from Singapore, Malaysia and the region. Since then, hundreds from this region have participated in the ministry of OM around the world, especially on OM ships. Unlike many from other parts of the world, the Singaporeans and Malaysians who joined the ship were able to do so with the recommended amount of money for their monthly support. Those of us from India had no support at all. Today, Singapore is a leading missionary sending nation.

Suddenly prohibited from having our programme in Indonesia. We had been praying and looking forward to entering Indonesia, a Muslim nation with a good size Christian population, with many who have turned to the Lord from Islam. On a previous visit, the Bible society sold out all their stock of Bibles. We enjoyed the large meetings, the long lines of people waiting to get on board and the beautiful churches with their large choirs. And it is a beautiful country. The advance preparation team had prepared the programme on shore and on board. We left Singapore on 20th May 1974 and arrived the next day in Jakarta, the capital of Indonesia, prepared for a long visit to its many port cities.

We were greatly shocked when we arrived in Jakarta and found out that our intended programme for the visit had been suddenly blocked by the religious department of the government of Indonesia, which was basically Muslim. To my knowledge, this was the first time we were denied permission to have a programme in a country. The ship leadership felt it was better to take the "No" as from the Lord rather than trying to persuade the government. A few programme line-up people were quickly sent off to prepare for the ship to visit to East Malaysia, and the Philippines, both to the north of Indonesia. The ship sailed the same day to Kuching in East Malaysia, about three day's voyage.

It was not till around 1990 that an OM ship was allowed back into Indonesia, and only to parts of the country which were largely Christian. A Muslim official would be present in all our meetings held on board for the local people. In God's providence, together with my wife, daughter and son, I was on board the second OM ship, the Doulos for this return visit.

Warm welcome in East Malaysia and the Philippines. We had a great welcome in the two ports in East Malaysia (Kuching and Sibu), and four ports in the Philippines (Iloilo, Bacolod, Iligan and Manila). Now looking back, this was God's way of expanding the work of OM further east and opening the way for many Filipinos to serve in world missions with us in OM and beyond. We were able to serve the people of these countries with much needed literature and also challenge them to fulfil their part in finishing the task of world missions. The Philippines is a major mission player today. Filipinos go, especially as tent makers into some of the countries that are more difficult to reach with the Gospel of the Lord Jesus Christ. There is an OM ministry in the Philippines today, recruiting and sending workers to OM ships and several other OM fields and a range of ministry in the Philippines.

OM ships have always enjoyed a wide open door to the Philippines since the first visit in 1972. I was not on board on that visit but I have heard how President Ferdinand Marcos and his wife Imelda Marcos together with their youngest daughter accepted the invitation to be Guest of Honour and to open the ship's book exhibition and its programme to the public. After a brief observation of the ship people (over 114 people from nearly 25 nationalities) living and working together in obvious harmony, the President paid us a great compliment. He said: "you are like the United Nations, except that you are united." The President's visit was nationally televised and this opened up the whole country for future visits.

God does not waste manpower. I enjoyed my visit to East Malaysia and the Philippines. There was a wide open door for evangelism and ministry to believers. Most people on the ship had a practical job for eight hours each day, mostly during the daytime but some worked shifts, round the clock in the engine or deck department. I was among the few whose job was full time (for lack of a better expression) in direct ministry. I did help out when all hands are needed, like the loading of hundreds of tons of literature which occurred in every few ports.

I have the impression most people were happy with the job they were assigned on the ship. I remember well the cheerful German cook Alfred Bosbach, the happy carpenter Gunner from Denmark, and the dedicated 2nd engineer Dave Thomas in his greasy overalls. George Miley, the Logos director used to say something like this: "God has given all the gifts, talents and skills needed in the body of Christ to enable us to build His Kingdom. The leader's role is to see that the gifts and skills are matched with the need."

The ship leadership did their best to make sure that no gifts were wasted. Often people were given roles which they themselves did not think they had the gifting for, but they ended up blossoming through them and making great contributions for world missions. Initially it could be very stretching. Sometimes it was like throwing someone into deep water where they had to learn to swim or sink. But the leaders were not far away. I learnt that God does not waste manpower. Neither should we. We should all be in the business of developing people, even stretching people to go beyond their present level of performance.

Distribution of a million tracts. Towards the end of our stay in the Philippines, the leadership realised that a lot of the one million Gospel tracts meant for the Philippines were yet to be distributed. If I remember correctly, we only had three days to distribute them before we sailed to countries with other languages where these tracts could not be used. The ship's storage space was not big enough for us to keep them for the next visit to the Philippines.

George Miley called me to his office - he wanted me to distribute the tracts in the Philippines within the given few days. In those days we never thought anything was impossible. Well, I went around the ship talking to department heads and individuals and got them going in all directions throughout the Philippines. Some went on planes, others on ships, and others by road. The Philippines is made up of thousands of islands. Some of the imaginative ones got on local Christian radio stations and told pastors that they could collect tracts for their church use. God in His mercy enabled us to distribute them or entrust them to responsible people.

A gracious Captain I did not realise that it was illegal for any of the 43 Logos crew members, whose job involved the safety of the ship, to be sent outside the city limits of where the ship was docked. The captain only knew what happened after they were gone. He went and questioned the director George Miley, who then sent me to see the captain. So with fear and trembling I headed towards the captain's office-cum-cabin.

Captain George Paget, the 70 plus year old gentleman from England, had lived and worked around India for most of his life. He was a man highly respected by port authorities around the Indian coast. They knew him as Captain "holy Paget" because he would not take bribes or give bribes and his paperwork was always in order. He was also known as the man who reads "the big black book" the Bible. Most captains could have "chopped your head off" for what I did. I expected something close to that. To my surprise, when I apologised, he said, "Well, God is Sovereign, He will overrule." Then he went on to make me a cup of English tea. And God did overrule.

The Logos in Saigon, South Vietnam, August 1974 The evidences of the war were visible as we sailed up the river Saigon, littered with all kinds of abandoned wrecks, helicopters and burnt-out army vehicles. Gun shots could be heard. Every night during our three week stay we would be woken up by the sound of a blast every two hours. "The frogmen" from the Navy would set off an explosive under the ship regularly to make sure the enemy did not attach a bomb to the hull of the Logos. The ship was well received in the country.

One of my jobs here was to lead a large team out to the city and give away 30,000 Gospels of Luke, donated to the ship by one of the Bible societies. We positioned ourselves by the traffic lights at the crossroads in downtown Saigon. It was exciting to give them away, as bicycles, in their hundreds were stopping for the red lights. All the Gospel portions were given away in a week or so. We did not know that this would be the last opportunity for open evangelism - the nation fell to the communists shortly after we left the city. The book Logos Story reports that 500,000 pieces of Christian literature were distributed during that visit. This included the Gospel tracts. What a privilege to be a part of such ministry, at such crucial hour.

Cambodia The ship was not able to visit this needy country where the people were hungry for the Gospel. An urgent plea came from the missionaries that we go over while the door was still open. The ship promised to send a team instead. The team was made up of David Teo from Singapore and Marcus Chacko and I from India. This is what David Teo wrote about it in a recent email:

"It was mid-August 1974. The MV Logos had sailed up the Mekong River to Saigon (now Ho Chi Minh City) for the first time, even as the Vietnam War was raging 40 km from the city. One week into the program in Saigon, George Miley (Logos Ship Director) in response to an urgent call dispatched a team to neighbouring Cambodia. The team, comprising Chacko (Team Leader), Marcus (from India) and David Teo (from Singapore), flew from Saigon to Phnom Penh and stayed at the Christian Missionary Alliance (CMA) Guest House. Food was scarce as Cambodia was in the midst of the Khmer Rouge insurgency and our meals were meagre."

We conducted an evangelism seminar for two days, attended by a few dozen young people. We had theory in the mornings and practical work in the afternoons, when we spread out all over the town for evangelism. There were four monks who attended to gain exposure to English conversation. In the process they indicated that they wanted to receive Christ. We also spoke at the Varsity Christian Fellowship, and shared testimonies with the three CMA American missionaries.

David continues: "Our time in Cambodia testifies to the goodness of the Lord. First, we were shocked to discover that due to an oversight we had no return visa back to Saigon. On the second evening, after prayer, we decided to go for a walk. David chanced upon a Singapore flag flying and behold it was the Singapore Embassy. Thank God the Singapore Embassy helped secure return visas from the Vietnamese Embassy the next day and gratis for the three of us.

"Second, on our walk back to the Guest House, we realized Marcus was missing. We turned back and found he had fallen into a manhole. Thank God Marcus was not injured. We later joked that for a brief moment we thought Marcus was "Raptured" and we were left behind.

"Third, a novice monk who came to the Varsity Christian Fellowship meeting sought out David and asked to accept Jesus Christ as his Saviour. Fourth, despite the wars raging in Vietnam and Cambodia, God's protection was upon us throughout our time in these places." This was just before the country became closed to the Gospel, followed by the severe persecution of Christians.

Bangkok, Thailand August 30- September 16. The next stop for Logos was Thailand, a land officially open to the Gospel but spiritually very resistant, where the people regard their king as a god. Bangkok means the city of temples. Buddhist temples, with large statues of Buddha, in golden colours are seen everywhere. The spiritual opposition was evident as we went about evangelising and ministering to believers. It is going to take a lot of prayer to see this country come through to the Lord.

Many missions, especially OMF (Overseas Missionary Fellowship) have been concentrating on this country for many years and churches are being planted. Praise the Lord. The OM ships made many return visits to this country. We were glad to meet a leading Christian businessman who on the ship's previous visit had donated one ton of rice and a large quantity of sugar to the ship. He is now with the Lord. He is one of those who have blessed us with various items including produce from their farms, like apples, sheep, fish and so on for our consumption.

Reach U.P.74 The month of October is the main changeover period for OM, especially for the OM ship. Many from Europe and America would leave or join the ship around this time. It was decided that the ship would sail to the Gulf and pick up the new recruits who would come overland from Europe. The same vehicles could then be used by those going back to Europe, for their overland journey. It was decided that my time would be better used in India, than at sea and in the Gulf States. George Miley suggested that I fly to India to represent the ship people who were to join the winter OM India evangelistic thrust. This programme was to be in the largest and most unreached state of India called U.P. The programme was named "Reach U.P. 74." About 30 ship people joined the U.P 74 teams a few weeks after my arrival. They disembarked when the ship docked briefly in Bombay.

Most of the OM India teams left their particular states at that time and converged on U.P. for a three month programme. It started with an orientation conference in Lucknow, followed by about 2 months of outreach and concluded with the All India OM annual conference. There were well over 30 teams of about 6 people in each team. Literature had been sent to each of the bases where the teams would be located. The idea was to saturate UP with Gospel literature and open air preaching. It also exposed the young people from all over India to the spiritual needs of the state. God blessed this programme, in answer to the prayer of God's people all over the world.

So the teams were spread out all over UP, the most populated state of India and the home of the most holy places and pilgrimage centres of Hindus. The state also has a high percentage of Muslims. The percentage of Christians was the lowest in India. In many places, professing Christians were going back to Hinduism. However, we encountered little opposition, and the word of God, especially in printed form, was going out all over UP. We had teams of ladies and teams of men. Men and women always worked in separate teams because of the cultural setting. I was one of the team leaders and drivers. They were exciting months. OM did a repeat of it the following year - called "Reach UP 75". The emphasis was on follow-up of the previous outreach.

Beyond the Natural

Saw my father for the last time. I rejoined the ship Logos in Cochin, Kerala about 70 km north of my home. This was around February 1975. My father and brother visited the Logos, enjoyed an extensive tour of the ship and had some idea of the work I was doing. It helped my dad to be at peace with how the Lord had been leading me, even though many had been telling him I was wasting my life. But I did not realise that this would be the last time I would see my father on this side of eternity.

Ship itinerary. I stayed on the ship for the next eight months, most of it away from India, and the Lord opened up new countries for our ministry. We were seeing many come to the Lord. Many Christians were catching a vision for missions, participating in prayer, giving and many eventually joined OM. This was the beginning of OM having permanent offices in many countries. I don't want to give long lists of port cities the Logos visited but it may be helpful to have a list of the ports visited during this period, to give you an idea of the ship itinerary. The dates indicate the time the ship spent in each port and the intervals indicate the time spent sailing to the next port.

Cochin, India	7 February - 28 February 1975
Visakhapatnam, India	4 March - 30 March
Port Kelang, Malaysia	4 April – 14 April
Singapore	15 April – 29 April
Kuching, East Malaysia	1 May – 10 May
B S Begawan, Brunei	12 May – 18 May
Kota Kinabalu, East Malaysia	19 May - 26 May
Zambuanga, Philippines	28 May – 6 June
Bacolod, Philippines	7 June – 16 June
Cebu, Philippines	17 June – 24 June
Keelung, Taiwan	28 June – 15 July
Inchon, South Korea	18 July – 8 August
Kobe, Japan	11 August – 28 August
Hong Kong	3 September – 12 September
Singapore	18 September – 22 September
Colombo, Sri Lanka	30 September 1975.

Notice how many different languages, cultures and religious settings the ship people had to adjust to in just eight months as they sought to minister in these countries. Before arrival at each port, an orientation would be given to the ship people about the cultural differences, so that we did not unnecessarily offend the people we came to serve.

"How to be effective for God in another culture" was a session given by George Miley. The principles covered were applicable for any country or culture we visited. The main emphasis of it was to love and accept people who are different from you. The accuracy of what I reproduce below is only as good as my recollection:

All cultures have good and bad elements in them.

Look at the positive things in other cultures and talk about them.

Ignore the negative things in other cultures, don't dwell on them.

Do not compare the best of your culture with the worst of other cultures.

The Lord Jesus encountered cultural prejudices from others (e.g. being from Nazareth).

Be ready for cultural prejudices against you.

Learn to forgive and not to retaliate.

Have a servant attitude: Philippians 2:3-11.

What he taught us helped me in my interaction with others. Even before the session, God had been impressing on me that all human beings are created in His image (Genesis 1:26-27), and all humanity comes from one blood – see Acts 17: 26 and Genesis 3:20 – a reference to Adam and Eve. Believers are one in Christ (Gal:3:28-29), and we should overcome all barriers to true fellowship.

On Indian soil again

Months of preparation had been going on for the second outreach in Uttar Pradesh, for Reach UP 75. Just as for Reach UP 74, most of the OM teams from all over India gathered together in UP for three months of united evangelistic effort. The Logos had promised to send a large number of its people to be part of UP 75.

Overland from Colombo to Lucknow for Reach UP 75. When the ship docked in Colombo, about 40 of us disembarked from the Logos to join our brethren in U.P. We had to travel overland from Colombo to Lucknow in UP, North India, which is nearly the length of India plus Sri Lanka. We expected border clearance when leaving Sri Lanka and also on entering India to be a nightmare which they were. We were delayed.

What Radha remembers from that occasion is the Indian customs officer pouring out the contents of her suitcase on the floor and she just stood there and cried. Em Namuco came to console her, made sure the customs officer did not steal anything, and helped repack the suitcase. The customs officer asked for a few things from the suitcase including a sari (must be for his wife). Radha acceded to his requests to get rid of him. The customs and immigrations in India have changed a lot since, for the better. So don't be afraid to visit India.

The train nearly left without us. We had to be in Madras at a particular time to board a particular train to Delhi which carried one coach specially booked for us for the trip to Lucknow. About 30 OM India people working in South Indian teams joined us in the Lucknow coach in Madras. The train would have left without the ship people, were it not for David Hicks who managed to persuade the railway station manager to delay the train and wait for us.

After waiting for quite some time and still not seeing the Logos team, the station manager decided to let the train go without us. Just as the train moved slowly forward, we showed up at the station. Dave Hick's lookout man ran and informed him. The green light suddenly went red. The train stopped and we boarded the train in record time.

Rajendran's father had travelled many hours and waited a long time in order to meet his son at the railway station in Madras, but they did not manage to connect. Upon arrival, we had to board the train quickly and the train left immediately. And there were hundreds of people on the platform, sending off passengers on the long train.

Reach UP 75. Well, there I was in Lucknow, the capital of UP state. The orientation week was held in a Catholic centre which had rooms for large meetings and accommodation for about three hundred or more people. We all brought our own sleeping gear except for Radha. She was a new recruit, had recently joined the ship and was on her way to work in India for two years. She thought beds and towels would be provided. To her surprise she found herself sleeping on cardboard and without blankets. It was winter. Not the best of conditions for a Singaporean. On the third day, one of the new recruits from Canada heard about her plight and gave her one of her two sleeping bags.

At the end of the orientation week, most of us were divided into teams of six or more to be sent into all the districts of UP. Each team had a leader, a driver with a truck or a van and translators who could translate into Hindi, the main language of UP. Each team consisted of a mixture of seasoned OMers and new recruits. OM mechanics were on hand for any repairs needed for the old vehicles. Gospel literature was sent ahead to the main locations where the teams would be based. After a week of teaching, much prayer and preparation, the teams were sent off. Unlike

UP 74 a year earlier, I had no team to lead. I was one of a few who were to visit the teams and minister to them and be with them.

All the teams were sent off and I was given my assignment of where I should start my visitation of the teams. There I was, in the OM base in Lucknow, all packed and ready to go, but I had no peace to leave. I must have delayed for a few hours and it was getting dark, when I was handed a letter by the OM person in charge of the post for the hundreds of OMers then in UP. It had arrived that day in the office. It was from my brother. My father had passed away. It meant that was the end of my participation in UP 75, and perhaps my ministry. The letter had been posted five days earlier. It took another four days for me to get to Kottayam, Kerala by the next available train.

On October 2nd 1975, my father passed away at the age of 52, just nine years after my mother passed away. Shortly before he fell ill, the Lord spoke to him to get his "house in order" and that He was going to take him to heaven. So he called my sister back from OM to arrange her marriage. She had served with OM in Karnataka state, south India for nearly two years and was about 22 years old. Within days of her return home, a proposal came from a pastor from the same district, Kottayam. He had been serving the Lord in north India.

Marrying off the daughters, including finding a husband for her, is the role of the father. Dad managed to fulfil it. In fact, he lived long enough to see his first grand child. At the time of his passing away, she was with her husband to Meerut, in UP State. Many years later, when my sister visited Kerala, a man with the gift of prophecy, who did not know us or our father, said to her, "Your father died after having committed all his children to the Lord in tears." This I believe.

My brother was 16 years old when our father died. He had visited dad that morning in the hospital before going to school. A few hours later, at about 3pm, someone came to the school and told him father was in a very serious condition and had been taken back to the house. When my brother reached home, father had died and there were many people gathered there, including church members. It has been painful for me to think of my brother having to face the whole thing alone, without our sister or my presence. As usual, he rose up to the occasion by the grace of God and the support of His people. As was the custom in those days in Kerala, father was buried within 24 hours, on the next day. At that time in the hot weather of Kerala there was no facility to preserve the body for the days before burial.

During my visit home earlier in the year, father apparently knew his time of departure from this earth was near. I now understand why he told me, "If ever a marriage proposal comes for you, accept it." This is not the way things are done in my culture. In Kerala's arranged marriage system he was the one who should see to it that I got married, which included finding me a wife. He knew he would not be around to do so. As my brief stay came to an end, unlike previous occasions, he called for our pastor (Pastor K.P.Oommen) to come to our home to pray and send me off. Father prayed first, weeping throughout his prayer.

Home to Kerala to see my brother. Concerned for my brother, I got on the first possible train heading south. Among my earthly possessions, all in a small suitcase, was a song book. For three days on the train, I was singing with tears. The death of my father was more painful for me than the loss of my mother. Father had shielded me from many who did not believe in what I was doing. To them, "going around distributing tracts and selling books" is not ministry. Father himself struggled for a couple of years with the thought that I did not know what I was doing, and in one sense he was right. Eventually the Lord assured him that I was in His will and he was at peace, perhaps uneasy peace. In Kerala, the children's future is a father's duty and pride. My parents were childless for nine years and had dedicated me to the Lord before my birth. They wanted me to go through Bible College, followed by a "proper" ministry as a pastor and a convention speaker.

Ministry days over? Having come home, I thought my ministry days with OM were over. However, my brother, just 16, and doing his final year in high school, insisted I continue with God's call for my life – that he could manage the property with its few coconut trees, beetle nut trees, black pepper plants, the few coffee plants and so on. I had taught him to drive and he now has "every driving licence possible". He was able to make a good living. Subsequently, he even had the offer of managing vehicles for a businessman - which he turned down so that he could go for full time ministry. Six years after my father's death, in 1981, the Lord also gave him a great wife. At about age 46, he decided to serve God, pioneering a good work in north India. My brother and my sister are among my few heroes. God's work of grace in them was deep. They are among the unsung heroes of our world.

All India conference Being assured by my brother, I left for Lucknow and joined the month long annual All India Conference of OM India. This was a time for the teams scattered throughout India to regroup and renew fellowship with one another and for the leaders to relate with the brethren. It was an important time of much teaching from the Scriptures, prayer, enhancing unity and planning for the future. I always looked forward to it, since my first one in Patna in 1967. George Verwer was willing to invest much resource for an event like this, knowing its potential. India has reaped its benefit ever since.

The All India Conference 1975 was coming to an end. Many from the south would be staying on in the north, and a smaller team would return south to recruit more brethren who would again be sent to the north. Many would be leaving OM for studies, joining other ministries or taking on secular employment. God desires committed Christians in secular employment too.

Where does the Lord want me next? Everyone knew where they were going except me. I had not heard from the ship about rejoining them. I was not even sure if I should expect an invitation to return to the ship. The fact I had been with the Logos for so long was an exception to OM India policy. I was very troubled. In a day or two everyone would have left the conference. That night, right after the evening meeting, Ray Eicher who was one of two coordinators of OM India wanted to see me.

Teaching study seminars OM India needed one more Bible teacher, preferably an Indian who could travel with John Brown, a Bible teacher from Northern Ireland. OM India was divided into three regions. If I remember correctly, the brethren would come together for two weeks of "Study Seminars" after every ten weeks out in evangelism. When Ray suggested that I be one of the two teachers for the study seminars, a dark cloud left my brain. I was at peace and welcomed the opportunity to minister to OMers from all over India.

I taught Jeremiah from the Old Testament and 2nd Corinthians from the New Testament. I was given textbooks produced by TAFTEE, (a Theological Education by Extension programme in India) and I was supervised by David Householder, an American serving at the time with OM India. It was a joy to teach OM India workers.

John stayed on in India for many years, eventually overseeing the work of OM in the north east, which consists of the four states of UP, Bihar, Bengal and Orissa - the biggest population centres of India. Radha Nair who later became my wife was in the group I taught in Bangalore. She was one of the leaders of the "Girl's Teams" serving in Karnataka. I had no idea, neither did she at the time, that within two years, the Lord would join us together for life.

Come Over to Europe

I was not in the habit of planning for my future ministry. I left the planning to God and just made myself available to Him. I was glad to have a role in India with OM. This was where my heart was. At that juncture, I received a letter from George Miley asking me to rejoin the Logos in Spain.

Difficulty getting a new passport. I needed a new passport, but the passport officer in Bombay would not issue it. I think he wanted a bribe. While the OM office at Bombay was looking into the issue of my new passport, I joined a small team to do follow up work for the evangelistic crusade meetings held every night for three weeks at Ludhiana, Punjab.

The number attending the meetings grew from a few hundred to many thousands and towards the end, the estimate was 100,000 people. The preacher, Rev. Jennings, was a Methodist evangelist from the USA. He conducted a healing ministry together with clear preaching of the Gospel. It was very moving to see all the Sikh people in their turbans and beards saying "Hallelujah!" after the preacher.

After preaching Jesus and the good news, he would pray for the sick and cast out demons, commanding the sickness and demons to leave in the name of Jesus. Hundreds, mostly women, ran to the stage and were instantly set free from demon possession. Many came forward to testify of healing. A man who was healed of a fracture from an accident invited us to his home for tea. God did something remarkable in this state, using this and many other ministries so that today Punjab is the only state in India that has at least one Christian in every village. I understand that this state has one of the fastest growing churches in India.

At the end of those wonderful evangelistic meetings, I joined the OM work at Ajmeer, Rajasthan. I stayed with a lively Tamil family who were doing church planting in Ajmeer. They were a breath of fresh air in a state largely unresponsive to the Gospel. They sang over and over a new song with a wonderful tune:

I will sing unto the Lord as long as I live,
I will sing praise to my God while I have my being
My meditation of Him shall be sweet,
I will be glad, I will be glad in the Lord.
 Chorus: Bless thou the Lord oh my soul, praise ye the Lord
(repeat 4 times)

Lord, how long shall I fast? Another thing I remember from that time is that I decided to do three days of fasting and prayer. On the evening of the second day of fasting, I was walking back and forth on the terrace and praying. I asked in prayer, "How long shall I fast Lord?" I expected the answer: three days. I was shocked when I heard in my ears: 21 days. It was too late to back off. I do not think I had ever fasted more than three days. I told the Lord, "Only, if you give me the grace to do so, Lord". I did experience the Lord's gracious enabling, and had a wonderful time with God and the Scriptures.

I had a long shopping list for the Lord, but going back to the Logos was not one of them. Late one night I was unable to sleep and was sitting and praying. I asked the Lord, "Lord, what about that invitation to re-join the Logos?" I was not expecting any response. The words came to me clearly (in my ears or brain): "No man forbidding him." I knew they were the last words of Acts 28 (KJV).

The Lord did enable me to complete the 21 days of fasting, but apparently, I did all the wrong things in the way I broke my fast. That evening, there was some kind of celebration taking place in the house. They were eating Biriyani, a beef dish with rice and spice in it. I ate a big plate full, with lots of meat. I did not know one should break fast slowly, starting with soup or easily digestible food. I also drank chemically flavoured acidic drinks throughout the three weeks – I wasn't aware this was totally inappropriate. I should have been in big trouble. Instead the Lord has continued to bless me with a good stomach till today.

No man forbidding him On finishing the fast I returned to Bombay for further instructions, and discovered that some kind OM person had done all the paperwork and got me a new passport. All I needed was to book an air-ticket from Bombay to London to join the Logos, which by now was in Dublin, Ireland. On the third day, I boarded the plane to London for my first ever visit to the West. I had heard about the cold weather in England and I was fully armed. I think I had more warm clothes on me and under my arm than all the other passengers on the plane put together (an exaggeration of course). I arrived in London in July 1976, the hottest July in four decades, just as hot as it was in Bombay. I should have carried some pickles or banana chips instead, or six months supply of rice. Indian restaurants were almost unheard of in those days in UK or Europe.

Back on the Logos in Ireland I rejoined the Logos in Dublin, Ireland. The cultural adjustment to the West was hard. I am thankful to George Miley for patiently seeing me through those early weeks on the ship. I wonder what he thought of my silly struggles. He had made the bigger adjustment of coming from America to Bihar and Bengal. So also did the hundreds of Westerners who came to OM India in the 1960s, 70s and 80s. The simple lifestyle of the foreigners in the teams was a huge testimony to believers in India. Their life spoke more than their preaching - sleeping on the floor, eating at cheap (therefore dirty) roadside restaurants, eating what the Indian team members were eating etc. George Miley did have one 'luxury' - he did carry with him a big container of peanut butter made in Calcutta. Peanut butter on dry chapatti and rolled with a banana in it tastes very good.

Ports in north Europe. We visited many ports in north Europe during the next five months. One of my ministries in the conferences on the ship, in Asia as well in any other place since, was to lead believers in these countries in prayer for spiritually needy countries of the world like India, China, Nepal, Bangladesh, Turkey etc. Prayer of the whole church is crucial for the advancement of the Gospel and prayer has made a huge difference to our world in the last few decades. I was also given short-term teams to lead for ministry with the churches.

Sheila Bowditch The most memorable church team I went on was in Scotland. Sheila Bowditch was the contact person from the church. A teacher by profession, Sheila was a committed Christian with many responsibilities in the church, including Sunday school. Well, she had us visit her Sunday school class before the Sunday service and after that class supported me for a good while. Their weekly collection was sent to the OM UK office. The bigger blessing was when she joined the ship Doulos in 1978, after my second visit to her church. When I challenged her to join the Doulos, she gave me many good reasons why she should not. The main one was the many responsibilities she had in the church and that there was none who could take over these responsibilities. I suggested that several people could shoulder them, one responsibility each. She was a major mover and shaker on the OM ships for many years. Sheila means queenly, and the name suited her well.

Rev. Dr. Quek Swee Hwa In December of 1976, the ship was in Brussels, Belgium. One of the Singaporean young ladies serving on the ship asked me to drive her pastor, his wife and family to the train station at four in the morning. Her pastor, Dr. Quek Swee Hwa with his wife and two little daughters had been on board to visit her and to minister on the ship. I did not know that he was also the pastor of Radha Nair who was serving with OM India at the time. All I remember of that early morning is that it was dark, very cold and the streets of Brussels were deserted. I did not realise the significant way

God would eventually use this pastor and his church in my life and ministry, especially in financial support from his congregation, for more than 32 years now.

The Second Ship Team OM had been praying for three years for a bigger and more suitable ship for the OM ministry. There were so many port cities open to the ship ministry and we only had one ship, which in those days visited about 15 ports a year. Most of that time was given to Asia. There was a sense we were nearing the time when God would answer our prayers for a second ship. George Miley asked me to be among about 40 people to stay back in Europe while the ship went down to Africa and on to Asia.

Our team of 40 was made up of many senior people, including some of those needed to run the new ship. George took us off the Logos because he wanted to give Logos time and space to develop a new team of leaders. The new ship, the MV Doulos, became a reality ten months later in October.

We were to take meetings all over Europe and the Americas. Frank Dietz was the leader of the team which stayed back in Holland. Joop Streetman was my roommate for six months. We preached all over Holland, with Joop both leading the team and interpreting for us. He went on to start OM Holland (Netherlands) and subsequently he became the OM area leader for northern Europe. He is now involved in leadership training. Also on the team was Annie, who later became Joop's wife. She was the team leader when Joop was not free to join us.

The most nerve-wrecking meeting took place in a church in Belgium. I was to preach at the last of a series of three meetings and Annie was my interpreter. Frank Dietz and Mike Stachura had taken the other two meetings. They only told me to prepare a message on relationship. When we got to the parsonage for a meal before the meeting, the pastor took one look at me, a 26-year-old, skinny, single man, and he asked Annie in Dutch, "Does he know what he is to speak on tonight?" I responded confidently, "Yes, on relationship."

The pastor panicked. He said, "no, this is a meeting for married couples, all newly converted from Roman Catholicism. They are having marital problems because they believe that as born again believers they should live like the priests and nuns, abstaining from sexual relationships."

The Lord helped me. I had 30 minutes to prepare while the meeting went on. All I could do was refer to verses on marriage from Genesis to Revelation. It did help that it was a period in my life when I was reading 60 chapters of the Bible a day. At the end of the service the pastor said, "The message has been recorded and will be given to the two couples who did not come to the meeting." God is gracious. Perhaps singles find it easier to preach messages on marriage because it looks simple and straightforward. From the feedback of the Belgian pastor, I could see that referring to the relevant passages in the Scriptures was an extremely important part of the message.

God loves to give rice too. It was in late January 1977. I joined Frank Dietz and two others to take meetings in Norway in a small town on the border with Sweden. It was a very cold winter and we were living with our hosts. For the whole week we did not have rice. We had all types of bread with goat cheese, ham and stuff like that. I never had a week when I ate so much bread in my life. By the fourth day, when I saw bread, my whole body began to tremble. Finally the week was over. The meetings went well and we were heading back to Holland. I insisted that we must eat some rice and curry somewhere along the way. We were in a Swedish town when we spotted a Chinese restaurant. Frank was not pleased with my request. He was handling the team finance and was worried about the cost as eating in a Chinese restaurant would not be cheap. But he too likes rice, having been in Asia for many years. Having a Filipino team-mate who also missed rice helped.

When we marched into the restaurant it was snowing. We had our simple rice and curry dish for the four of us for 60 Swedish Kronas - quite expensive for us in OM in those days. But the rice never tasted so good. When we reached the car, we noticed some papers stuck under the windscreen wiper. It was 120 Swedish Kronas. I looked around but there was not a soul in sight. The town was deserted due to the heavy snow. Well, our God, He understands human feelings.

George Verwer: During this time in Europe I visited an OM Conference held at the Belgium Bible Institute. It must have been a tea break every one was out in the grounds of the institute. George Verwer walked by and after a couple of sentences the next thing he said to me, almost out of the blue, was that he prays "more for wisdom than anything else, in fact, the only other thing I pray for more is love." Looking back it was prophetic, a word from the Lord to me. Can we pray too much for either of it, wisdom or love? I wish I could tell you that I took full notice of it and practiced it ever since. I am afraid not.

Europe to India in an old OM van

In June of 1977 Frank asked me to drive an OM van from Belgium to New Delhi, India, with two other drivers – Walter, a Swiss mechanic and Noel an American missionary to Holland. The van was loaded with books and other evangelistic tools to be delivered to countries en-route to India. The old Ford diesel van which was painted pink had been fixed up by our mechanics based in Zaventum, Belgium. It was meant for one of the girls' teams in OM India for their evangelistic ministry. The 10,000 km drive took us 21 days. We drove non-stop, except for about 15 forced stops to fix an air leak in the fuel system.

A Prank Fire Our mechanic decided he would fix the problem for good. We were in Turkey, having travelled through Belgium, Germany, Austria, Yugoslavia and Greece. We found a deserted area where we could work on the van. There were a couple of Turkish youngsters hanging around. As I was exhausted, I slept. Noel kept watch while Walter went under the vehicle to check the fuel system. He lowered the tank and some diesel spilt on the ground. I was awakened from my deep sleep by a loud scream: "Chacko, come out quick!" The mischievous youngsters had set fire to the fuel on the ground under the van! I crawled out of the van and joined Walter and Noel to push the van away from harm's way. The air leak problem was fully fixed and we drove for hundreds of miles across Turkey without any further problem.

God anticipates our needs. We were in a town in eastern Turkey and Walter was driving. I was beside him and Noel was asleep in the back. The road was so bad that Walter decided to shift down into first gear. As he did so, the gear stick snapped inside the gear box and became embedded about two centimetres inside the box. Walter continued to drive in first gear till we were clearly out of town. He then stopped the van by the side of the road, dismantled the gear box and retrieved the broken piece of gear stick.

Just then a tractor approached us. The three of us could not speak a word of Turkish but when Walter showed the driver the gear stick and the broken piece, he understood that it needed welding. He signalled Walter to get on the tractor with him and drove Walter to a welding shop. The shop had just opened two weeks earlier. It was run by a Turk who was trained in Germany and he spoke fluent German, which was Walter's language. He actually did the welding for us free. Thankfully, we had no more mechanical troubles till we reached New Delhi, our destination. We were deeply grateful to the Lord for the way He undertook for us throughout the journey, including the last stretch through Iran, Afghanistan, Pakistan and finally India.

India was a huge shock to Walter and Noel. While Walter did not say much about "the culture shock" of what he saw and heard in India, Noel was outspoken. I wonder what would have happened if Noel had flown straight into India without the benefit of gradually getting used to the many cultures we encountered along the way. As it was, he was thoroughly shaken up by the poverty and idolatry in India and he flew back to Holland. He kept saying, "I could not have imagined this condition in my dreams."

Walter stayed in India for about two years, serving from the OM mechanics base in Delhi. He fixed up about 40 old vehicles (all British) used by the OM teams all over India. Our Pink Panther, as we called our van, because it was painted pink, also entered the Lord's service. It was used by one of the OM girls' teams in India for several years.

To Bangalore. In July 1977, after the overland trip, I met up in Bangalore with Frank and Anneli Dietz and their daughter Amy, and my roommate in Holland, Joop Strietman. We ministered together for three months all over India. This was Joop's first trip to India, and he had a great time. He went back to Holland to marry Annie in the fall of 1977. Joop and Annie have visited India many times since and they have helped to mobilise significant financial and prayer support from Holland for the work of OM India.

God did not want me to settle down in India Knowing my desire to serve in India, George Miley wrote to Alfy Franks with the proposal that I be based in Bombay (OM headquarter at the time), and work all over India with OM "as Alfy's eyes and ears". The matter had to be discussed with the OM state leaders from all over India. Frank Dietz, Joop and I were invited to attend the All India state leaders meeting held in Tumkur, and some time during the week, the topic of my return to OM India came up for discussion. Alfy presented George Miley's proposal to the meeting.

There was not much of a discussion. One of the leaders who had been with OM India for a long time said, "If Chacko is joining, I am leaving." There was a silence. Frank Dietz eventually broke the silence saying, "If you do not want Chacko, I will take him back to the Logos." The silence continued. And then the discussion moved on to other subjects. I did not know it then, but God had other plans for me.

I remained in OM India for another four months. I participated in the "MP Penetration Plan." Much like UP 74 programme, it was an all India OM programme in the state of Madhya Pradesh (MP). There were many boys' teams and girls' teams all over MP and we flooded MP state with Gospel literature. My team leader was Madhusudan Das from Orissa. He was a good leader and preacher as well as a good cook. I was the team driver.

Baptism. During this time, two young people wanted me to baptise them. One of them was a final year student for the Roman Catholic priesthood. I objected in vain, saying it was too cold, as it was the winter of 1977, and that before a believer is baptised, he should have joined a local fellowship. Well, they were baptised in a cold river in Ujjain, MP. Praise God that both have been serving the Lord in different ways. The ex-priest started a mission, bringing many tribal people to faith in the Lord.

The other was Edward Amanna. He was still in his teens. He had turned to the Lord after overhearing an OMer sharing the Gospel with another man. When the man refused to receive the Lord, Edward leaned forward and said, "I would like to receive Christ into my heart." Edward, a very skilful and gifted motor mechanic, stayed on with OM for many years, eventually leading the team of OM mechanics who took care of the 40 vehicles used by OM teams all over India. Today he is a successful businessman.

The snake slithered away. On a summer day I visited two Indian missionaries in north Bihar. One of them told me that there were two graduates there who had been studying the life of the Lord Jesus for about seven years. They had many questions about the Bible. He then asked me if I could spend some time with them. I readily agreed and met up with the two young men the same afternoon. We went to a large open space and sat down on the dry ground and I started to answer their many questions.

About two hours later, having answered most of their questions as clearly as I could, I went on to share my testimony with them as to how I came to put my trust in the Lord Jesus Christ as my personal Saviour and God. I emphasised to them the Lord Jesus must be their only God and Saviour and not just one more of the many gods they believe in. In fact they were told that they should tell the Lord Jesus they were forsaking all their former gods. They agreed to do so.

I gave them the option to go home and think through the matter and then make that decision at home and invite the Lord Jesus to be their personal Saviour in the way I had done or they could pray to the Lord right there and then. One of them replied that he had been waiting for this moment for seven years and he did not want to wait any further. The other young man agreed. They then repeated a 'sinner's prayer' after me. As they prayed, "Lord Jesus we forsake all our former gods and receive you as our only God and Saviour," I heard a big snake slither away from where we were sitting. I opened my eyes in shock, as there were no bushes or grass nearby and I did not expect the presence of any snake. The two of them were apparently oblivious to what had taken place. We carried on with the prayer, and they accepted the Lord Jesus as their personal Saviour and Lord.

When I went home, I sought the Lord to understand the meaning of the sound of the snake slithering away. The answer came to me, "Therefore if anyone is in Christ, he is a new creature; the old things passed away; behold, new things have come" (2 Cor 5:17). To me it meant the Lord Jesus had entered their heart and a spiritual transaction had taken place. When we truly repent and trust the Lord Jesus as our personal Saviour and Lord, something takes place in the spiritual realm. This is true whether we experience something obviously spectacular or not. The Bible declares: "Whoever will call on the name of the Lord will be saved" (Rom 10: 13, cf. Acts 20:38, Rev. 12:9).

My brother Another highlight of these four months in India was that my brother joined me for a month. He learned driving at this time in Ujjain and returned home with his first driving licence. I put him on a special programme. He joined us in all the team activities which included several hours of evangelism, and he read through the New Testament in 30 days. He had a sense of purpose and accomplishment. The Lord lit a fire in him for soul winning. Today, it is still burning - brighter than ever.

Marriage I was 29 years of age and still single. I knew I did not have the gift for celibacy. But I also did not have the means to get married. I was a volunteer with OM with no salary and it was not suitable to carry on living out of a suitcase as a married couple. My future in OM was as shaky as a house on sand. OM was a short term movement. It has been a training movement. The majority of people in OM move on.

Beyond the Natural

A poor Indian pastor told me to trust God. When he was single, the Lord met all his needs as a single man. When he got married God met all the needs of both of them. Now they have several children and God was still all-sufficient for them.

George Verwer apparently had instructed Frank Dietz to find me a wife while he was in India. Frank asked the English lady (Joan Beasley) who oversaw the OM ladies work in India for a recommendation. Three names were given to Frank. He never told me about the first two, but said, "The more I think about it, the bell is ringing for Radha Nair." Radha is from Singapore, a Hindu background believer, a medical social worker and was leading an OM India Girls team in Karnataka. I had heard about her from others and apparently she had been told about me too. We met and Frank gave us the OM social permission to discuss if the Lord was in it.

Radha told me one of her conditions for marriage was that her father and pastor would give full consent. Radha's pastor, Dr. Quek Swee Hwa, visited her parents and recommended me. Surprisingly, she got the "all clear", although her father, a police inspector in Singapore, was not yet a believer in the Lord. He came to the Lord about 12 years later, at aged 72, nine years before he went to be with the Lord in 1990. It was an amazing conversion story in which various ones including our children (his grandchildren) and I played a part. My children prayed daily for his conversion. Radha's mother, three brothers and three sisters were following the Lord already.

Radha had almost completed her two year commitment with OM India and would be flying off to Singapore from Bombay. We met at the OM national office in Nana Chowk, Bombay (subsequently shifted to Hyderabad). I popped the question, "What do you sense the Lord is saying about this relationship?" She replied, "I do not have peace about it."

In the course of our brief talk I mentioned what I read that morning in my quiet time: "Do not be afraid, O daughter of Zion, see your King is coming, seated on a donkey's colt" (John 12:15). Then she told me that was also her reading for the day. Zion is the name of her church, but I did not know at that time. We left the door open for the Lord to lead us according to His will through further confirmations.

Alfy Franks, one of the two national leaders, who has earned himself a reputation for matchmaking in OM India, suggested that we get engaged during the all night prayer meeting. He knew Radha was leaving the next day or so. Maybe this was the push we needed. So, at midnight during the prayer meeting, Radha and I, together with another prospective couple, K.Rajendran and Pramila Samuel, got engaged. We celebrated the occasion with Indian chai (tea) and laddu (an Indian sweet), which was broken into two halves to multiply it for all the 20 to 25 people in the prayer meeting.

An Indian brother felt very sorry for us, because there were no engagement rings and no money for refreshments. Many Indians have the superstitious belief that this is a bad omen and it would mean terrible shortage of money for the entire married life. However, the Lord has met all our needs for the past 32 years. Rajendran and Pramila got married shortly after the engagement, and I had the honour of being the speaker at their wedding. Radha returned to Singapore in October 1977, soon after the engagement.

Doulos enters the Lord's service with OM I remember being on the Logos when George Verwer visited the ship people in one of the Scandinavian ports. OM had been praying for another ship for about three years. One day, I overheard George Verwer saying to George Miley, "Unless we see a major financial breakthrough we are going to have to abandon the idea of a second ship." What a joy it was for me that same evening, hearing it being announced that Youth with a Mission was giving the money they had set aside for their first ship to OM. We could go ahead with the second ship project. It was a very big gift and was a clear sign from God that OM should not abandon the ship project. However, it was another year before all the necessary money came together and the second ship was purchased.

In October of 1977, George Miley and several senior crew members agreed to buy the "Franca C" from a ships scrap yard in Italy. They had just enough money to pay for the ship. This purchase of the ship was an answer to the prayers of many in different parts of the world. But it would be another seven months before I would see it for the first time. I remember George Miley showing a Franca C brochure and explaining how the ship could be used. The ship was three times bigger than the Logos and had more space for meeting rooms and the book exhibition. In addition, it had superior accommodation for the ship's people, with a toilet and a bath attached to most cabins. The cabins were bigger than the Logos's tiny cabins. Franca C was a luxury liner!

The first six months of its life with OM were spent into refurbishing it to suit our purposes. Apart from the engine, another major job was covering up the ship's swimming pool so that we could use the surface area for a huge book display, and the space below for book storage. It became the biggest floating book exhibition in the world. The only other one was the Logos.

At Home in Singapore

Singapore I left Bombay and arrived in Singapore in late February 1978 to prepare for my wedding six weeks later in April. Radha and her father met me at the airport. I had twenty pounds sterling (£20) in my pocket, thanks to John Brown.

I stayed at the OM office and became the OM leader of Singapore. The post was vacant after Frankie Low, the previous leader, left for studies. Some months later, Rodney Hui, who was in Bangladesh at the time, took over the leadership.

On my first Sunday in Singapore in Radha's church, Pastor Quek Swee Hwa came by while we were having fellowship tea, after the service. He asked me, "Are you supported?" I said, "No." Then he asked, "Do you mind if we support you?" I said, "No." He made a quick note, and said, "I will talk to the elders and let you know next Sunday." I did not expect anything to transpire from these brief few words. I was wrong.

Well, that was the beginning of Zion B-P Church, and the pastor in particular, supporting us. During the weeks that followed, Pastor Quek gave us some premarital counselling and helped us plan the wedding service. He even drove us around to buy the wedding rings and make catering arrangements.

Recruiting for OM ships. I was in Singapore for four months, from the end of February till the end of June 1978. While there I was given the responsibility of recruiting Singaporeans, Malaysians, Indonesians, Filipinos and Thai people for the work of OM, and in particular, for the OM ships, Logos and the new Doulos. I managed to recruit 67 people for a year commitment to work with OM and all of them were fully supported by their respective churches. Lawrence Tong from Singapore, Meggy Pelupessy from Indonesia and Boon Siang from Thailand were among them.

It was not as difficult as it may sound, as I had been given 400 commitment forms - with names and addresses of people from all these countries. They had attended mission conferences on the Logos when the ship was in their ports, and each one had made a commitment to missions, filled a form and signed it. I just needed to follow them up, by post, telephone calls and personal meetings.

However, it was also not so straightforward. In different ways the evil one tried to prevent various ones from fulfilling their commitment – accidents, job promotions... but God is sovereign. Perhaps He led some to other missions and He may want many to remain in the market places as effective ambassadors for Christ. There is a desperate need for strong Christians in the job market. I have heard of an accountant who, when asked, "Who are you?" replied, "I am a Christian thinly disguised as an accountant." Amen to that!

Newly married Radha and I were married in Singapore on 8 April 1978. Pastor Quek officiated at the wedding. It was also a commissioning service. Written across the front of the sanctuary were the words "So send I you", taken from John 20:21. We became the official missionaries of Zion. Since then, many more have joined the ranks. George Miley and my former Logos room-mate for six months, brother Jordan Khan (a Bible teacher and evangelist now with the Lord) participated in the wedding service, with Jordan Khan preaching a long message in his closing prayer. He was one of the signatories on our wedding certificate.

In God's providence, Logos was in Singapore. This made it possible for many of my old friends to attend the wedding. Radha's friends from Navigators organised the reception and the chief cook from the Logos made a lovely wedding cake. Radha and I drove to Cameron Highlands in Malaysia for our honeymoon in an OM Volkswagen Beetle. We recruited the "resort" owner's son and his fiancé to join the Doulos for a year. I think we took a couple of meetings too.

In early July, Radha and I accompanied the 67 new recruits to Belgium for the OM orientation conference. Jonathan McRostie, the OM leader for Europe met us at the airport. Handing them over to Jonathan ended my responsibility. The new recruits participated in the summer campaign all over Europe, after which, they were assigned to different OM fields. Many of the recruits from SE Asia joined us on the Doulos to finish off their year commitment, with a few of them extending their commitment. Lawrence Tong is still with OM, serving in leadership roles.

*Chacko is (in the second line from the back, nearer the captain)
in this picture of Logos in Glasgow in 1976.*

A usual sight of visitors to the Logos II

On OM Ship Doulos in Latin America

Joining Doulos in Spain in 1978 July 9th. Radha and I, together with an Indonesian recruit Meggy Pelupessy joined Dale Rhoton and his family in a VW van and drove from Belgium through France to Bilbao, Spain to join OM's newly acquired second ship, the Doulos. Doulos is a Greek word meaning "bondservant". Meggy subsequently pioneered the OM work in Indonesia and led it very successfully for many years. Many from Indonesia joined OM as a result.

A beautiful cabin in the mid-ship was set apart for us (better for sailing in rough seas). It was originally a four bunk bed cabin. They had removed the beds and intended to build a sofa cum double bed for us so that during the day it would be a living room and at night a bedroom. But with all the pressing jobs around the ship, the carpenters overlooked our need. It was almost a month later that they became aware we were sleeping in our sleeping bags on the floor. The ship's floor was not flat like our floors at home - it was curved. We had no idea where in the cabin we would wake up the next morning - it would not be where we went to bed. When François Vosloo, the chief carpenter, heard about it, he apologised and soon we had a bed.

Besides bread we had porridge for breakfast. And the leftover porridge was added to the soup in the evening meal. For the first week on the Doulos we had no rice. Then we had rice for an evening meal. So we went over to the Norwegian chief cook and thanked him for the rice. After that we had plenty of rice. It was written on the entrance to the Galley (kitchen) that "complaining against the cook is hazardous to your health". A whole chapter could be written about food. Suffice to say, I had never had apples in curry prior to that – and why not? Lots of apples were given to the ship by local believers, and they appeared in just about every menu, including the curry.

Busy Conference Co-ordinator. Radha and I had been married for three months. We were now part of a huge community of 350 people and Doulos became our home for the next five years. Radha was the librarian and in charge of on-shore meetings to be taken by the ship's women. I was the conference co-ordinator. We had many conferences on board, sometimes two or three a day. Some key conferences like those for pastors may last three days. I had a small team to help me. I enjoyed this responsibility very much and relinquished it reluctantly when I was asked to move into another role after a year.

I must add that it was a taxing job. I was basically on my feet all-day. Many nights I would come to my cabin, and would lie down with a few pillows under my feet. I remember one day in Swansea, Wales, six months into my conference ministry, I was standing at the entrance of the Main Lounge, as it was called, where the large conferences that can take more than 300 people took place. One of the first people to return from the coffee break into the meeting room was an older man, a retired pastor. He took a look at me and said, "You need a break. I want you to come with me." I told him that I am a married man and he said, "Come with your wife." Well, I delegated my jobs quickly and joined this dear man who took us to his wife and home and gave us just the break we needed. It was my first break on the ship, a great three days. It kept me going for another six months.

They were an incredible five years for us. I preached in more conferences in those five years than in any other five-year period of my life. Usually the themes of the messages were: the Lordship of Christ, world missions, prayer for the world, discipleship and leadership. I could repeat my messages as we were in different ports every three or four weeks.

My favourite message was the one based on Isaiah 6:1-9. I got the three points from a line in one of AW Tozer's books: the upward vision, the inward vision and the outward vision. The first, the upward vision, spoke about a vision of God ("I saw the Lord..."), the second was the resultant vision in one's heart ("woe is me...") and the third the result of a vision of God and having been touched by Him - the vision of a lost world (whom shall I send and who will go for us" to the lost world.) I usually ended the Scripture reading with the first part of verse 9: "He said, Go..." The ship was uniquely equipped to fulfil the role of mission mobiliser, although it could also adapt to other roles as needed.

I served in three different roles on board: conference co-ordinator for a year, personnel director for two years and associate director of Doulos with specific responsibility for training, also for two years. Preaching, however remained as my main function. George Miley invited a large number of OM and Logos long termers to join the Doulos – to fulfil the ministry aspect and also the crew. This was a wise decision as it made the launching of the Doulos ministry easier. George Miley was the first director of Doulos as well as the general director of OM ships. I consider him a great international leader. After a year or so, he and Hanna moved to Germany as the general director for both the ships, a role he had handled on the Doulos. His moving out meant a major leadership shuffle on board.

An unlikely Personnel Director. The most difficult and the most rewarding job I was given on the Doulos was the role of personnel director. Frank Dietz who did it before me, besides being an American with a loud voice, was known to be "rough and tough and hard to bluff". People could imagine him doing the job, but not me. We were 350 people from over 40 countries. I never anticipated this job, so never sought to understand it, although by then I had been on the two ships for a total of about six years. Frank had been the personnel director the whole time. It took about six months for me to get a handle on the job. It was all "on the job training". Sink or swim was the idea. In those days there were no formal training manuals for such jobs, which OM ships have today.

It happened in this way. There I was, at the height of my enjoyment of the conference ministry and I was very happy with the results. I was commended for my work by George Verwer, George Miley and others. The ship was ministering in Rio de Janeiro, Brazil when I was asked to take over as personnel director. Brazil has many ports and we always had great programmes there. (The ship had already been to several ports in Great Britain and Europe, a port in the Portuguese island of Madeira in the Atlantic Ocean, then two on the east coast of the USA and again two ports in Mexico.)

One day, Frank called me to his office and told me that he and his wife and daughter were going on a short holiday. A rich Brazilian lawyer had offered his huge house in the countryside, beautifully situated on a hill. Frank wanted Radha and me to join them. I was told that Em Namuco who had been part of the conference team would take over the conferences. Em was a missionary with New Tribe Mission in the Philippines. He was a natural MC (Master of Ceremonies), talented in music, a good speaker and could even dance. He had been with the OM ships for more than four years.

Frank then told me he would be leaving the ship for a long break to minister in the USA and Finland and he wanted me to take over the personnel responsibility on the Doulos. So we went on our second holiday. Soon after we arrived there, Frank pulled out the personnel list of the Doulos. He then went over each name on the list and said something about each person while I scribbled the information on paper. Three days later we were back on the ship and it was announced to the ship brethren that I would be the new personnel director. I felt as though the whole ship was thinking "he won't make it".

Invest in faithful men: 2 Timothy 2:2 I sought to do my best for the job, which meant I worked very long hours. Anyone could see me any time of the day or night. Imagine 350 people on the ship with you day and night. I was like a headless chicken. Then something happened that changed my approach to the job. A young Malaysian who had completed his time (a year) on the ship came into my office to say goodbye to me. He mentioned that I had contributed to his life and he was very thankful. He was one of those who basically looked after themselves, followed the rules, did the work given and made the best use of the opportunities to grow and serve.

It dawned on me that I had been devoting most of my time to a small group of people, who benefited little from it, and they contributed little to the ship ministry. And here was this young man who contributed much to the ship ministry and benefited much from the little time I spent with him. I decided to seek out such people and make sure that they had time with the leadership in smaller groups, besides a few other things like reading of certain materials for the week or times of prayer. This approach fitted in well with one of the goals of the ship ministry – the training and development of the personnel. In the process, I was able to delegate my job to six part time helpers who took charge of the routine personnel needs. I appreciate the good advice of Jethro, the father-in-law of Moses, who advised him to delegate.

Frank, Anneli and family returned to the ship and he headed up the training department and was the associate director while I stayed on as personnel director. Obviously I did not sink, I was swimming. Looking back over the years, this is one of the more rewarding periods in my life. I learned much and was able to impact many for the Lord and missions. Early in 1981, Dale Rhoton who had replaced George Miley for two years, also went to Germany to the ships headquarters to assist George oversee ship ministry. Frank Dietz took over as Director and I had to pass on my job to Em Namuco. I was given Frank's role as the director of training, and associate director, a key pastoral role. It is awesome to have a part in God's training of people who will eventually serve Him all over the world.

The Doulos in Latin America George Miley and his large leadership team were very sure we were going to Latin America for just about one year: December 1978 – September 1979 - starting in Mexico and then the ports on the east coast of South America. OM had no work in Latin America except for Mexico which was the first OM field. They had no plan to expand the work into Latin America. We decided to limit the Doulos visits to Mexico, Argentina and Brazil. Our first two ports of call in 1979 were the Mexican ports of Tampico and Veracruz. Many key people like Juan Daniel Espitia of Mexico, Daniel Bianchi of Argentina and Humberto Aragao of Brazil were among the early recruits to the Doulos. Our eyes were opened to the missionary potential of Latin America - God wanted us to be missions mobilisers.

We saw a continent with a fast growing church, more evangelised than Europe, yet a church that still thought of Latin America a mission field and was calling for missionaries to come over to them from Europe and North America. We told them: "You are not a mission field but a missionary sending continent." We presented specifically the challenge of Southern Europe, North Africa and the Indian subcontinent. Our emphases for the churches of Latin America were: discipleship, leadership and world evangelisation. We talked about the countries in the 10/40 window although they were not yet named as such. Much time in conferences were spent in prayer for these nations. Prayer for these nations is the best way to impart mission vision.

Of course the opportunities for evangelism were always at hand. Ray Lentzsch from the USA was leading teams daily from the ship into the streets for open-air meetings and hundreds were turning to the Lord in every port. There was one port in northern Brazil where one thousand people professed faith in Christ in one month. We were challenged by the first line of a song we were singing in the weekly Prayer Night on the ship. The song was: "O for a thousand tongues to sing". It became a suggestion and a prayer request - and the ship people especially Ray Lentzsch embraced the challenge. At the last count of the decision cards, there were a few more than 1000. I am not vouching that they were all born again. God alone knows the actual number.

Believers in these countries were powerfully used of God in the harvesting of souls. The evangelical church had been growing slowly for decades since the beginning of the 20th century. The momentum was building up and people were hungry for the Saviour. However, evangelism was not the primary reason for our being there. We would rather be like the Apostle Paul, preaching where Jesus was not named. And such a ministry needed a huge army of workers - Latin America had many sons and daughters who should be among them.

The hundreds of conferences on board the Doulos all over Latin American ports as well as "Operation World Conferences" held inland in cities were aimed at mission mobilisation. We had pastors in small groups to come and live on board so that they could interact with the ship people from 40 nations - some of whom had come from spiritually needy nations of the world like southern Europe, North Africa and Asia. It fell on me to lead these groups. And we had some able people on board who had had exposure to many unreached nations of the world and could give first hand information. We pored over the pages of the great mission handbook "Operation World" and prayed for specific nations. God was planting a vision for the unreached peoples in the hearts of the brethren in Latin America. A ship with 350 people can make a huge impact.

But all this was not enough. It needed to be followed up by action. So we recruited directly from Latin America to the ship, although there were no OM offices in these countries at the time to process the applications and to be responsible for those who joined the ship. At any one time there could be up to 60 Latinos on board working among the 350 OMers from about 40 Nations. Then we started to select people from them to take with the ship and drop off for three months in Spain and Portugal for the evangelistic outreach, specially organised with these recruits in mind. On the ship's return to South America, more young people would join us. This was a helpful exposure for the brethren from Latin America to the needs in other parts of the world.

Recruits from British ports. During our short return to Europe (October 1979-March 1980), mostly for ministry among believers in northern Europe, 40 Latinos went to Spain and Portugal for the

OM evangelistic campaign. As a result, we often found ourselves short of people. Peter Maiden was the OM UK director (presently the international director of OM) and he gave us the freedom to recruit British people from the UK ports we visited. We made known during the conferences on board we were in need of recruits, and the types of people we were looking for.

Anyone interested could simply pick up a duplicated sheet of paper giving the details and see me. This was an exception to the way OM usually recruits people; so we had other steps in place, including an interview with the pastor or elder of the applicant's church. We recruited about 12 British people in a few weeks and they were just as good as those who came through the best recruiting process we had. I am glad to say there were no casualties among them. God did undertake. One of the strengths of the ship was the large number of senior people who could look after the newcomers. After the short visit to Europe the ship returned to Latin America.

Miracle in Callao, Peru. Decio de Carvalho was among the first to join the Doulos from Latin America. He later became one of the line-up people who went ahead of the ship to ports and countries to prepare the ship's visit and programme. He reminded me recently about a major answer to prayer. He wrote "Dick Dueck and I did the line up there in Callao. Do you remember what happened there? There was an article of the Constitution of Peru that prohibited any nationals from going aboard a foreign ship. The authorities there told us the only solution was to change the Constitution. God led us to a man who prepared a proposal to be presented to the National Congress to amend the Constitution. It was passed, and finally signed into law by the President on the day the ship arrived in Callao. All in three months!"

Latin Missionaries. Decio went on to be the first national leader of OM Brazil, later a misionary to Turkey with his wife and family. Today he is the executive director of COMIBAM, an umbrella organisation for mission in all Latin America. Thank God for the thousands of Latin missionaries now serving all over the world with many Latin mission organisations as well as with OM and other international organisations. There are more than 200 Latinos serving in India and many more making short-term mission visits, especially people from Mexico and Central America.

I am thankful to the Lord for granting me the privilege of contributing something to this development through my eight years with Doulos in Latin America. The Lord Jesus exhorts us to "ask the Lord of the harvest to send out more workers". Fewer workers, less harvest. More workers, more harvest. We need many workers to work together to finish the task of world evangelisation.

One way to have some idea of the Doulos ministry is to look at the statistics. And here, gleaned from the Doulos story, are statistics for a few ports in Latin America:

Number of visitors to the ship:
Callao, Peru (September 1980) 148,864
Veracruz, Mexico (February 1982) 160,246.

Ports with the highest attendance at on-board programmes:

Callao, Peru (September 1980) 25,000
Belem, Brazil (September 1981) 27,000
Mar del Plata (January 1981) 27,800
Rosario, Argentina (April 1981) 30,000

The Doulos Story gives other details including the number of countries and ports visited, and the number of Bibles, Christian and educational books sold in each port - they make a staggering read. They indicate the effectiveness of the OM ships in world evangelisation and also help us appreciate the stress the ship people endured in those days. The leadership did their best to provide some privacy to the ones not involved in the event at a given time. For example, the ship's children could go to their school on board without meeting any of the visitors.

On home leave in Singapore

By August 1980, Radha and I had been on the Doulos for slightly more than two years. We had ministered in 58 ports, some of them twice over. We had already circumnavigated the South American continent, and we were beginning the second round. The ship was in Salvador, the fourth port in Brazil, heading up north on the east coast of the continent, having come down the west coast of Chile. Radha was nearly two months away from giving birth to our daughter Sheela. If we stayed on with the ship she would have been born in Puerto Rico, but we wanted Sheela to be on her mother's passport, and be a Singaporean. For that to happen, Sheela had to be born in Singapore.

George Miley kindly allowed us to take a much-needed break in Singapore. I had to remain on the Doulos till the end of the Brazil visit so Radha had to leave by herself before the airline's seven month cut off point for pregnant women to fly. There was a shortage of leaders and preachers on the ship during that period because some of the leaders had gone to Europe for the OM annual conference.

The suitcase. Radha needed a good suitcase for the trip, and as usual, we prayed about it. On Sunday, we were asked to join a church team and preach in one of the churches on shore. After the meeting, a couple invited us to their home for lunch. As soon as we arrived, the man disappeared into the house and reappeared with a suitcase - just the kind we would have liked to have for Radha's journey to Singapore.

He said, "While you were preaching, the Lord told me to give you this suitcase." We were blessed, knowing that the Lord knew our need and had provided. Radha left within a day or two for Singapore and stayed with her parents.

The Chief Justice of Brazil. I discovered I had overstayed 80 days in Brazil. I had asked for a 90 day visa for Brazil and presumed the immigration officer had granted it to me. Thankfully the Chief Purser, who was working on other passports decided to give me my passport too, although my departure was not immediate. He noticed that I had overstayed my visa as they had only given me 10 days and not 90. We sailed to the next port of ministry, Belem, and hoped that the problem would be simple and could be sorted out by the ship's agent. But no one would touch my passport. In those days, to overstay in Brazil was a crime punishable by imprisonment. They would arrest me when I went through the immigration in order to leave for Singapore.

Rafael Lopez, one of the Brazilian pastors who joined the ship and had been helping to line-up the ship's visit to Brazil, was on board. He called up a few people, got in touch with a congressman in the government, and learnt that only the Chief Justice could overrule in this matter. The Chief Justice was contacted and given the date of my departure and flight details. Well, I left Belem and flew to Rio de Janeiro airport to leave for London and Singapore. As I went through the immigration counter (as advised), the immigration officer was taken aback when he saw that I had overstayed. I could see the expression of shock on his face. Just then a man dressed in a suit, who had been standing behind him as I came through, stepped forward and handed a piece of paper to the officer. Soon my passport was stamped and I could go out of the country.

Reporting back to our sending church. I arrived in Singapore and was glad to meet up with Radha, her family and church friends. During my meeting with Pastor Quek, he advised me to open a bank account. This was because the church wanted to put a small amount of money each month into this account. He was aware that our support money went straight to OM and that we had no other income. This monthly giving was a huge blessing to us whenever we returned to Singapore for short periods. Thank God for generous people which meant we never had a shortage in Singapore.

This visit to Singapore was an important time to renew our links with the church particularly with the leadership, the pastor, elders and deacons. We were the church's fulltime missionaries. We were among the first then, unlike today when they have many serving in several countries, from Albania to Japan. We thank God for a church with a strong mission's vision, which gives half of its income for missions. It is strong in local and foreign missions. The senior pastor, Dr. Quek Swee Hwa spends much time taking its members on short term trips to mission fields like India and other places. The church has been a strong mission base. This I believe is what a local church should be. The church has supported us in OM for 32 years with no direct benefit to them. They see it as an investment in the kingdom of God.

Getting ready for the birth of our first child. One of Radha's brothers had offered to take us on a tour one Sunday afternoon to see the Bird Park in Singapore. When the time for the Sunday service came, Radha said she would not be going to the service. This was very unusual. So I went alone to church, and on my return she said she wouldn't join us for the Bird Park either. So I went with her brother. After seeing the beautiful Bird Park we headed for the Japanese Garden. However, we missed a turn and I suggested we go back home.

As soon as I got into the house, Radha said she needed to go to the hospital. So we called the doctor, our church elder, Dr. Quek Swee Peng, a well known gynaecologist in Singapore. On his advice, Radha was admitted into the maternity ward in Mt Alvernia Hospital, and Sheela was born within two hours of our arrival. Radha chose her name - it is Indian but not Hindu, and would be easier for her family to relate to, rather than a Christian name from Kerala or the West. It is an international name, so it has been easy for all, except it has the Indian spelling. I was glad I could be with Radha during the birth of our first child. I had no fatherly instincts until Sheela was born. I was changed instantly. In fact I did not sleep the whole night. Have you noticed that the God compares himself more with the fathers than with mothers?

A short visit home to India. God's timing is perfect. Five weeks after my daughter's birth my brother got married in Kerala, India on December 10, 1981. Being so close to India I was able to spend two to three weeks with him and enjoy a family reunion. The Lord gave him a young lady strong in the Word and prayer. I would say that she is a wise woman too. She was a pastor's daughter. Her father was greatly used of God and respected in their area. I pray for my brother daily - always with a heart of deep gratitude to God for His deep work of grace in him.

The Lord did not give them children. When the Lord called him in 2004, they moved to North India. They are now serving the Lord in UP, one of the most unreached states in India. He is a great pioneer. I can never support him enough. I have been praying much for two districts in UP: Ghaziabad where my brother is and Meerut where my sister is. Both are in church planting ministries. Their lives have been a great encouragement to me. It could have turned out very differently. My brother could have gone astray after our father's death. He once told me he wanted to live in a way that honours our parents. Thank God too for the godly influence of his pastor, Pastor K.P. Oommen.

Pastor K.P Oommen is now with the Lord. He kept my brother active in Sunday school and youth work and paved the way for his involvement in the denomination, and eventually coming out into full time service, in his mid forties. My memory of him is a tall and quiet man, only spoke when necessary. He would be remembered for leading us out to open air preaching Sunday after Sunday. He also built up a healthy, mixed caste congregation. The only phrase I remember hearing often from all my open airs with him is "People of all castes and religious are invited" to Christ or to the church.

Second term in Latin America

After my return to Singapore, nearly two months after Sheela's birth, we flew to rejoin the Doulos in Kingston Jamaica. It took us 70 hours: Singapore – Tokyo – Hawaii - Los Angeles - Florida – Jamaica. We did not have a US visa, and so we had an immigration officer assigned to us in each of the three US airports. This was a blessing in disguise, as the officer knew where to go in those huge airports and got us on the right flights. He also carried our luggage for us. My Indian passport was not the best to travel the world with, but it worked for 25 years. Radha and Sheela and later our son Sunil had Singapore passports and I made sure they were on top of the pile whenever I had to apply for visas. It worked each time - although in some Latin countries they thought Singapore was in China!

Mexico. We arrived on the Doulos in the first week of January 1982, at the tail end of its visit to Jamaica. By the time we had settled in, it was time to sail. The voyage from Jamaica to Coatzacoalcos, Mexico, was the roughest voyage I can remember. I thought it would be the last voyage of the ship. A few ships went down along this route, and one big ship washed ashore - we sailed past it on our way to the port. There have been a few other voyages since then which were almost as bad. I am glad to be alive to tell the story.

It was in this port that a bank employee, Fernando Garcia, came to the Lord. He is presently the OM leader of Mexico. Years later, on the ship Logos II, he was one of my right-hand men in leading the ship in Latin America. Our next port of call was a return visit to Veracruz, Mexico. This is the nearest port to Mexico City. Coach loads of people were coming to the ship and we were sending many teams inland to take meetings in the churches. Our conferences were full. Sheela, about three months old, had her first ice cream in Veracruz, when some of the Doulos ladies took her for an evening walk - it was Rum and Raisin! We visited a third port Tampico, before leaving Mexico. I did not know that this would be my last visit for a long time, till 2007 when Fernando invited me to speak at the OM summer campaign held in Zacatecas. I was back there again in Queretaro for another OM summer campaign in 2009. Mexicans have a heart for world missions and especially towards India.

USA Although not Latin America, since we were so close to the USA, we could not resist the opportunity to visit St. Petersburg, USA after a twelve day ministry in the Nassau, Bahamas. This was not Doulos' first ever visit to a US port. We did swing by Portsmouth, Richmond, USA (Nov 10 - 29th, 1978) on our way to Mexico in 1978. Portsmouth was the port where the ship was built in 1914 and it was also the home state of George Miley. Mrs Miley, George's mother, brought a lovely chair for him. He only used this solid office chair for two years before he passed it on to me, when it became necessary for him to direct the ships from a land base. I state this to emphasise the harmony I felt on this large international community. God had done a deep work in all of us that the natural barriers of race, status, nationality, denominations and all that have been overcome. We were one in Christ, it was a reality.

The USA had many supporters of OM and the ships, both in prayer and finance, besides parents and families of many of our people. It was an important opportunity to meet many of them and thank them. Among the many who ministered to us on the ship was Cliff Barrows (Billy Graham Evangelistic Association) and Dr Ralph Winter. This was the first time I had ever heard of "the people group" approach to missions. How significant an idea it has been since for evangelising our world!

South America. With Puerto Rico our next port of call, we embarked on ministry in the Spanish speaking world, except for a week in Curacao (Dutch). Apart from Brazil, almost all the Latin American countries are Spanish speaking. We reserved Brazil, a huge landmass on the north and east of the continent, for the end of the ship's itinerary.

Following a two week visit to Puerto Rico, which has one of the largest evangelical concentrations in the world, we spent two months visiting three ports in Venezuela. Evangelism was the priority here. The evangelicals were few, made up of small congregations, like little islands in the vast ocean of Roman Catholicism. We saw many turn to the Lord. We also had a special programme for pastors. Every week we had a fresh group of pastors live with us on board for a week. They participated in the spiritual activities of the ship like morning devotions, a few of the conferences and the weekly night of prayer, which went on till about 2 am. The main purpose of the programme was to encourage them and expose them to missions.

After short ministries in Barranquilla in Colombia and Bilbao in Panama, we went through the Panama Canal to minister in 11 port cities in Ecuador, Peru, Chile, Argentina and Uruguay. We left Puerto Rico on the 17th of May 1982 and 11 months later, we were in Montevideo in April 1983, the last of the Spanish speaking countries on the continent. The next ports in Brazil would be Portuguese speaking.

The Lord gave us a great ministry in these ports. The programme in each of the ports was about the same. It usually started with a port orientation for the programme staff and then for the whole ship. There would be a welcome programme for the local leaders who had assisted with the preparation for the ship's visit and an orientation meeting for local volunteers who helped out while the ship was in the port. The ship would be opened to the public by a local dignitary - we try to get the top person if possible, either the president or the governor. They usually cut a ribbon to open the book exhibition to the public and the exhibition would be open all day till about 10pm. In some countries like Argentina, we kept the book exhibition open till 2.00am.

The programme on the ship included conferences for pastors, ladies, youths, professionals and seminars on various topics like evangelism and marriage. Children are an important part of the ship ministry. Many schools send their children to spend an hour or more on the ship to look through the books and attend a programme for the children. We also sent teams to prisons and other institutions to minister to people on shore, besides taking hundreds of meetings in each port in churches and local gatherings, among them evangelistic rallies. Well, there are many ways to use a ship in ports. Let me move on to share some experiences that stayed with me from these ports.

Ecuador This is the country where the American missionaries were killed in the 60s, among them Jim Elliot. We ministered for a month in the ports of Manta and Guayaquil. I was able to take a short holiday with Radha and Sheela in Quito, the capital city, up in the mountains. We stayed in the home of a missionary with HCJB, the Christian radio station, first of its kind, broadcasting the good news all over the world. The missionaries had gone on a furlough and we had the house all to ourselves. Sheela was nearly a year old.

It was in this port that the small group of men and women, who had volunteered for an Intensive Training Programme lasting six months, did their all-day-hiking, one of the requirements of the programme. I decided to join them, being overall in charge of training on the ship. About 20 of us left early in the morning, walking till early afternoon. Most of it was in the hills. Then it was time to walk back to the ship. Our bodies were aching all over, from head to foot. Just as we reached the bottom of the gangway of the ship, we heard the bells for dinner on board the ship and I was told I would be preaching in an evangelistic rally. After a hot shower and a quick bite, I was driven to the meeting, getting there just in time to preach. Thank God, here and all over Latin America, it was a ready harvest.

Peru and the surprise visit of the President. Salaverry in the north and Callao in central Peru, near the capital Lima, were the two ports we visited in Peru. It was a Sunday early morning and most people were still in bed, except for some of the church teams getting ready to go for their meetings all over Callao and inland to Lima. The ship was closed to the public till 2.30pm. Some cars pulled up at the gangway of the ship, and a few people stepped out and walked to the gangway. The watchman Emtage from Barbados was about to finish his night shift. A gentleman introduced himself as the President of Peru. Emtage initially did not believe it but it was true. The ship leadership was alerted, including the Argentinean public relations officer, Ruth Cliff. Soon, a little party was organized. It included the director Frank Dietz and the captain Carl Issacson and his wife Marion. The book exhibition was opened up for the president and his party and they bought a large quantity of books. The president also invited the Captain and the ship people to visit his palace. About 40 of us, including the ship officers in their uniforms enjoyed the visit.

Sheela had her first birthday in Callao, Peru on the 1st of November. One day we left her with Melanie Allen, a bubbly teenager and daughter of the Doulos chief steward. When Radha and I came back Sheela said to us "Hallelujah". It was couple of months later in Chile that she took her first steps. In those days I was reading a couple of Christian joke books. I used to read them and laugh and Sheela would laugh with me. This may be the reason she loves reading so much. Sunil my second child was addicted to reading - he started to read from age one.

Chile Much happened in Chile, the next country, south of Peru. Four ports had been lined up for the visit in this long and narrow strip of land sandwiched between the Pacific Ocean and Argentina. The ports were Arica in the north, then Valparaiso which is also the port for Santiago, capital city of the country, then Talcahuano and lastly Punta Arenas. The one thing no one on the ship would forget is the prayers that went up for the reduction of the port fees for the four ports - it was US $250,000. In God's providence, President Pinochet was approached and he waived the whole fee. We stayed for two and half months in this country. OM today has an office and ministry in this country. Many from Chile have been serving the Lord with OM on the ships and in other countries.

The Pentecostal Methodist Churches of Chile. What an interesting combination. We enjoyed many meetings in these churches on Sundays throughout our stay in Chile. What impressed me was their singing. One church I went to had about 100 people, young and old, sitting on one side, each with an instrument that looked like a small guitar. They accompanied every congregational song during the service and it almost lifted the roof up. It gave a taste of heaven. I must say Spanish and Portuguese songs are very uplifting.

Molar Pregnancy. In Arica, our first Chilean port, Radha started to have complications with what we thought was a normal pregnancy. She was admitted to a military hospital where the doctors found no life in the womb and yet her womb was growing. It turned out to be a false pregnancy, known as molar pregnancy. It is rare in Chile but a bit more common in places like Singapore and Hong Kong. When the news was conveyed to Radha's brother, a medical doctor, he immediately called us on the ship to say that we should return to Singapore immediately for treatment. One of his friends was an authority on this illness and he gave Radha six months to live if not treated right away.

A D&C was done for Radha, and having confirmed that it was not malignant, we were able to stay on the ship a while longer. This was the beginning of the end of my five years with the Doulos and my ten years with the OM ships which had started in June 1973. I had also been thinking that it was time that I stop preaching about missions for a while, and be a missionary in Asia. I was particularly drawn towards India again, a country I was sharing about almost daily in our conferences on board the Doulos. Well, eventually after six moths of treatment for Radha in Singapore, we did go to India for the next three years.

Punta Arenas, our last port in Chile The scenery was breathtaking - beautiful mountains, trees, flowers and the sea. We were there in the last week of January, their summer, in 1983. Radha, Sheela and I were able to take a brief holiday here in the holiday home of a believer. We were never great holiday makers, and so we stayed home, appreciated the scenery, did a lot of reading and enjoyed Radha's cooking. Soon we set sail for Argentina, traversing treacherous southern waters which would claim OM's first ship Logos five years later in 1988. The Logos is still sitting down there on the rocks, the only ship that is still refusing to sink after hitting the rocks there.

Argentina There was a war going on between Argentina and Great Britain and many of the ship people were from UK. The British people were not allowed off the ship. Unlike previous or future visits, this was a short visit - just two small ports (Bahia Blanca and Mar del Plata) and only a month or so.

The Doulos was registered in Malta, a neutral nation. This made it easy for Doulos to enter most countries but individuals may face difficulties. I remember a coloured South African who was not allowed on shore in Singapore when we went there with the Logos in the early 1970s. He lamented, "In South Africa I am discriminated against because of my colour, and here it's because of my South African passport."

Many Argentineans came on board to attend the conferences and to buy books from the book exhibition. It was not easy for some Argentineans to listen to British preachers on board whose country was at war with theirs. But it was a time to show Christian love for one another. About ten years later, a visiting preacher on board, Dr. Tony Sargent preached in many conferences during that later visit to Argentina. At the end of one conference, a young man went to Tony and told him that he did not hear anything he preached because he was British. They were reconciled there and then. Tony told the young man that he would give the Malvinas (Falklands) back to Argentina if they would take Northern Ireland with it!

Again some years later, we had a British captain who used to serve in the British Navy. He was a specialist in weapons inspection. He told us that one day on the Falklands, after inspecting a bomb the Argentineans had dropped, he saw an American elderly lady walking down the road. He asked her, "What on earth brought you here?" She replied, "I looked on the map and thought this would be one place where they would not drop a bomb, and so I came to live here – but within weeks the war broke out." Well, as we have often heard, the safest place for us believers is in the centre of God's will.

I have always enjoyed my visits to Argentina. One of its states is called Chaco. They always laugh whenever I introduce myself. Initially I did not understand why they laughed. Many Argentineans responded to the missions challenge given by the Doulos ministry - some served for a few weeks as volunteers while the ship was in their port while others joined the Doulos for several months and some for years. This would be our last visit to Argentina as a family for a while. Ten years later we returned as a family of four and visited many ports in this beautiful country on Logos II for about six months.

It was not easy to say goodbye to the ship, especially to people like George Miley and Frank Dietz. In mid March our family of three left the ship in Montevideo, Uruguay. Many came with us to the airport for a final good bye. I was all in tears. However, it was symbolic that we left our base, the Doulos, in Latin America because it had been my main field of service for the last five years. What an incredible tool the ship has been for evangelism, mobilisation and training.

We were heading home to Singapore to an unknown future. It was one step at a time. A chorus that has ministered to me many times is:
"My Lord knows the way through the wilderness
All I have to do is follow.
Strength for today is mine all the way
And all I need for tomorrow.
My Lord knows the way through the wilderness
All I have to do is follow.

India Calls

Back to Singapore. The priority was for Radha to have her check-up and she had many hospital visits over the next few weeks. It was confirmed that her health was not in any danger. She just needed to visit the hospital annually for a few more years. During the short time in Singapore, we worked with our sending and supporting church and also with OM Singapore and Malaysia. OM India during this period had been preparing for a massive outreach in Bihar and UP states – the Ganges Outreach 83 (GO 83). It was a three-month long outreach in Bihar and UP, involving most of the OMers in India. The Ganges River, regarded by the Hindus as holy, flows through these states.

India calls. Radha and I discussed going back to India. She felt that for the needs of a family with a child, she would need a gas stove for cooking (instead of the normal kerosene stove which you have to pump and was not safe), and a fridge. I suggested we pray and commit the matter to the Lord. And the Lord did provide enough gifts in Singapore to cover both. I departed for India first (for GO 83), and left Radha and Sheela in Singapore with her parents, as Radha still needed clearance from the doctor.

How to find God? I was asked to be one of the preachers for the GO 83 programme. Marcos Chacko was the leader of this "Ministry Team", primarily working with the churches. One meeting stands out in my mind. We invited about a dozen Hindus who had completed the Bible correspondence course with a mission called the "Light of Life" to spend a whole day with us.

The topic for the first session was: "What is God like?" We knew what Hindus believe about their gods, salvation etc. This was the most important session of the day. The purpose of the session was primarily to give a Biblical understanding of God, which would also help the participants understand what sin is. It also prepared us for the forthcoming session on Jesus, the God-Man, Lord, Saviour and Judge. It was also necessary to emphasise the divine nature of the Lord Jesus.

I was very glad to see after my first session, one of the participants, an old Brahmin who was a headmaster of a school, went out and bought a full Bible from the bookstand we had set up. Instead of going for his tea break, he went straight back in and asked the OMer who sat with him during the session to help him locate the verses on God that we had referred to so that he could underline them in his new Bible. I knew the major work had been accomplished.

The second session "Why we are without God" was a study about man, from Genesis to Revelation. The Hindu view of man is very different. This study helped the participants see clearly why man cannot save himself. It prepared the way for the third session on the Lord Jesus Christ – the God-Man and His death for our sins – and why He alone can save us.

The final session on Salvation, besides dealing with the Biblical concept of salvation (which is very different from other religions), also explained the need for man's positive response to the Gospel message. This session ended with a call to invite the Lord Jesus into their lives. Every participant repeated the sinner's prayer, renounced allegiance to all other gods and affirmed their faith in the God of the Bible as their only God and Saviour. What a joy to hear them call God, the Creator of heaven and earth, "Our Heavenly Father".

Together again. Radha and Sheela, just turned two, joined me in Patna, the capital of Bihar. Our house was just a mile away from the

Ganges River. We had been drinking from a well in the compound of our rented house. Even though we filtered the water and boiled it, we were getting ill, especially my daughter, who suffered from amoebic dysentery. So we sent the water to the city authorities for a check. The result came back: "Not fit for human consumption". Unfortunately, we had no other option in those days but keep drinking it. These days you can buy bottled water in India.

After the three month programme of GO 83, we gathered in Gorakhpur for the annual All India (OM) Conference. From the first day of the conference, the main prayer need was for finance to cover the expenses of the conference, especially for the food needed for several hundred people. And there we were, sitting on some money for our gas stove and fridge. Finally Radha said, "Let us give it." We already had our ticket to fly to Bangalore, which became our base for the next three years.

Bangalore and God's wonderful provisions. We boarded the plane and Sheela was singing choruses to her heart's content and keeping herself occupied. The plane made a stopover in Hyderabad. A man from a few seats behind us came over to me just before the plane landed and handed me Rs.2000 - worth a lot more in those days. He said, "The Lord told me to give you this money. I told the Lord, 'I would give him Rs.500', but the Lord said, 'Give him Rs.2000.' So here it is, and no strings attached." We were assured the Lord would provide for all our needs.

At Bangalore, the first issue was accommodation, and the Lord graciously provided beyond our needs. A well known Indian evangelist Augustine Salins, sent for me. He was the weeping evangelist of India, the founder of Ambassadors for Christ which had its HQ in Bangalore. He had retired from the mission and was not in good health. His daughter wanted her parents to join her in Australia. When I met Mr. Salins, the dear man said, "I want you to live in my house, for a small rent to cover my expenses in India." When I looked around, I knew Radha would be pleased. We moved into the fully furnished house which had two gas stoves and a fridge freezer, and a garden with fruit trees!

Chitty Chitty Bang Bang. An American missionary lady who had brought her new car with her to India was retiring after 31 years. The car had clocked 30,000 miles and she and her husband wanted the car to remain in the Lord's work. Her husband told me there were people who wanted to buy it but they wanted me to have it - but they needed two air tickets from London to Atlanta. I checked with Edward Amanna who was my team member and an expert mechanic and he advised me to go for it. George Verwer in London kindly made the two tickets available for the missionaries and we had the first ever car in OM India. What a blessing the house and car were for those three years, especially because Radha, Sheela (and Sunil who was born two years later) suffered much ill health in India. God knows how to comfort us.

Ron and Lilo Penny. Radha was so blessed to have Lilo (German) live not too far from us, to have someone she can relate to and pray with. And for me, it was good to re-connect with Ron, my former boss in north India, now serving with the India Bible Society. One single blessing was that Ron got the Bible Society to print 30,000 copies of a booklet I wrote according to their requirements (70% of the content being quotes from the Bible). This was an evangelistic booklet called "Steps to knowing God."

Malabar Outreach I started off with a ministry team ministering to the churches and taking evangelistic meetings. Eventually I ended up being the South India coordinator for OM India. The job involved much travel in the south and also across India. The car was only for local use and mostly for the family. The first long distance we drove in it was to a Muslim outreach we had organised in the Malabar area of north Kerala State, which has a Muslim majority. A number of us including Radha, Sheela and Sunil, who was nearly a year old, got in and we started the long drive.

Preserved. We were on a nice road with big trees on both sides and very little traffic. I must have been driving at about 40 miles an hour, when the left tyre on the back burst and simultaneously the brakes also failed. I lost all control of the car, including the steering. Miraculously, the car made a perfect U-turn and stopped on the other side. It was as if a mighty strong person had stood in front of the car and restrained it. Sheela immediately burst into singing: "He saved my life (x3), He's so good to me" - to the tune of "God is so good" - a song she had heard many times. She was about four years old. Yes, the Lord had preserved our lives. It was a miracle. We decided to change all the tyres - they must have been the original tyres and tubes from 31 years ago! We did manage to get to the outreach, which the Lord blessed.

Operation World Conference. The Lord put on our hearts to organise an all India Missions conference in Bangalore. We called the conference Operation World, although the main emphasis was India. Our goal was to gather 300 keen Christian leaders from all over India for three days of prayer and the challenge of missions. My team member and friend Shankar and I visited Dr. Theodore Williams in Bangalore and explained our vision to him. He told us, "I am all for missions" and encouraged us. He was happy to serve as the chairman of the organising committee. We then visited Mrs Juliet Thomas also from Bangalore. She told us, "My answer to all committee requests is, no. But for OM I will do anything."

Rev. Theodore Williams threw his whole weight behind the Operation World conference. Without him we would not have had the calibre of people coming to the conference, but with his influence we gathered 300 key national Christian leaders. Alfy and Ray got the OM world, especially OM India, praying for the event. At that conference we challenged the leaders to pray and trust God for 10% of India to turn to the Lord. I have since upped the prayer to 20%. We are on the road to India becoming a Christian nation. God is able.

The Lord gave us a capable committee. Saji K John proved to be an able administrator for the event. K. Rajendran, now General Secretary for India Missions Association, and Phil Davis from the U.K., led the meetings. Frank Dietz from the USA and Alfy Franks, the then All India coordinator of OM India, were among the main speakers. Ray Eicher, also co-coordinator of OM India, led the prayer sessions – they were a very important part of the conference. Evangelisation of India was our heartbeat. We had a sense that the Lord would use the conference for that purpose.

The battle for Sunil. Sunil was born in 1985. We nearly lost him in the womb. During the early months of pregnancy, the doctors in Bangalore could not find any life in the womb and they had concluded that it was another molar pregnancy. More than one check indicated no life in the womb. So a date was set for the D&C. I drove Radha to the hospital. After a few minutes she came walking back to me and said that she requested them to do one final check before the D&C and it showed that there was life in the womb. Gracious Lord. And we would not have missed Sunil for anything in the world. However it was only the beginning of the battle for his life.

We returned to Singapore briefly for his birth so that Radha had the support of her parents and family, and returned to India soon after his birth. Radha and Sheela and now Sunil were plagued by various illnesses, in spite of all the precautions we took. All three were plagued by Asthma. It was much later that I leaned that Bangalore is "the asthma capital of India." It took me a long time, nearly three years, to see that India was not where the Lord wanted us. That happened in June 1986, just weeks after Sunil's first birthday, which we celebrated in Connor, Nilgiri Hills. One of the gifts for his birthday was a golden cross (it was prophetic).

We returned to Singapore even though we had no specific ministry offer. Foremost in my mind was to save my family, albeit late, as all three were terribly ill. I just had to accept it that my role for serving India would be from outside the country – mobilising prayer for India together with periodic ministry visits to the country. This understanding has since proved to be of God.

Handing the work over. I have never stayed too long in any one leadership position. The good part of that is that someone else, most of the time someone better than you takes over. Shankar, my right hand man in India, took over the role from me, and led the work with great effectiveness. Shankar and I first met in GO 83. He had been following the Lord for just a few years. He came to the Lord from a Hindu background. At college he was studying Milton's Paradise Lost, Paradise Regained." The old Hindu Professor said to the class that if you want to know more about it you should read the Bible.

Shankar searched for a Bible for a long time and finally found one in a second-hand bookshop. As he read the Bible, he became convinced that God is greater than the idols of Hinduism. He saw God's greatness in the creation story. A fellow student brought him to the Lord and his family accepted Shankar as one of their own. This was very helpful for the young believer to grow in the Lord. They prayed for him daily. On graduation, Shankar joined OM India, travelling all over and preaching the Gospel with the OM teams. Eventually he started to lead teams in his own state of Karnataka. By the time I met him he already had a year of experience on the Logos. The Lord used Shankar to see his parents and several of his brothers and sisters come to the Lord.

Assisting Shankar was another team member Kumar Swamy, who now leads the OM work in South India. Kumar, another able leader, is also from a Hindu background and has been with OM for many years. The work is now so much bigger than when I left it in 1986. Shankar has since left OM and is now concentrating on his state, mainly encouraging and helping first generation Christians. Many of them are in the ministry and the churches are multiplying. Karnataka is one of the most unreached states in south India. I have the privilege of working closely with Shankar in his Karnataka project. I often teach in the Bible conferences he conducts for first generation believers in the Lord.

Again back to Singapore. I left India on the 16th of June 1986 with Radha and the children. Our church (Zion Bible-Presbyterian Church), thank God for it, came to our rescue. I was given a pastoral role, pastoring a small congregation of 60. I also picked up a couple of years of studies at the denomination's Bible College. It was a significant time to be with the whole church for an extended time, as it deepened our fellowship with the church and strengthened our prayer and financial support base. We also needed a different pace from the one we had for more than eight years living with a large community. The Lord led us to rent a house, on the next street to Radha's parents, in the vicinity where she grew up. All these were factors for restoring the health of the family.

God shall supply all your needs. The rent of the house came to 500 Singapore dollars (S$). Our allowance was S$ 700. We decided that we would give the tithe of it to the church. So we had S$130 for all our expenses including food and transport for the month. But it was amazing how the Lord kept us going. There was a monthly postal order that came in our letter box from an anonymous giver. Every so often a church elder, Elder Heng, would come and stand next to me after the service. He would then quietly slip in a few dollars into my hand. Elder Heng, a business man, is now with the Lord. He was one of the founding elders of the church. "He was a good man" as pastor Quek wrote about him in the church bulletin.

We had no car but some friends and family would leave their cars with me when they went on business trip or on holidays. So often we had transport, a big help in hot and humid Singapore. By the way the rent was reduced S$450 within a short time. Every bit helped. We were aware the Lord was looking out for us.

News of the Logos shipwreck. On 5th January 1988, in Singapore, I heard the unexpected news that the Logos, OM's first ship, had hit the rocks in the notoriously treacherous waters of the Beagle channel, at the southern coast of Chile. I was surprised the news hit me so hard and saddened me so much. It was not just metal and wood. Five years of what the Lord did in me and through me was represented by that vessel. I had seen the birth of a vision, having prayed for the ship since 1967, as well as being part of it from 1973-1978.

It still is my favourite OM ship. I think I last saw her in 1978 in Singapore, when I got married to Radha and in God's providence the ship was in town. To me, that ship represents a mighty work God was doing all over the world, especially in Asia. Many OM offices in Asia and Europe would look back to it as their origin. What a vision the Lord gave to George Verwer - and the courage to make it happen! What a tool in the hands of the Lord!

Thank God for keeping all 139 on board safe. One group had to come down on a rope ladder. Imagine a young crew member coming down a rope ladder with one hand and with the other hand holding on to the captain's five month old son. Half way down the ladder he screamed, "I can't!" - He was told he had to, and he did. However, they lost everything except what they were wearing and their passports. The chief purser, Stan Thomson, had held on to the passports from the moment the Logos crashed on the rock, till all were evacuated about six hours later. The chief engineer, Dave Thomas was the last to abandon the ship. All the people were transferred to navy vessels and taken ashore.

When the news of the Logos shipwreck reached a church in Brazil where many of us had ministered over the years, Pastor Edison Queiroz announced to the congregation that: "The Logos was not just an OM ship. It was the ship of all Christians and it should be replaced." He then proceeded to take an offering for a replacement ship. This took place even before the OM leadership had time to think about a replacement ship. They did come round to it. A ship double the size of Logos was bought at the end of the same year and refitted with large ministry facilities and accommodation for 199 people. It was named Logos II.

The Logos had run its course. She had served the Lord for 18 years in all continents, visiting 258 different ports (revisiting many of them) in 103 countries. 3.5 million educational books and 1.6 million Christian books were sold on board, which included 450,000 Bibles and New Testaments. Countless tracts were distributed on shore. More than 7 million people visited the ship. More than 4,000 people served on board, and benefited from a training programme for them. All these were accomplished through a second hand ship bought for £70,500!

It was a beautiful ship. It was incredible that OM in those days could afford it. And perhaps even more remarkable was the way the Lord undertook for the finance needed to keep it sailing, especially with the ever increasing price of the fuel needed for the ship.

Spiritual warfare and the Lord's work One day, during this period in Singapore, the Lord led me to fast and pray for several countries surrounding Singapore, which included much of Asia. I was specifically praying against the forces of darkness and false beliefs which kept the people in bondage, and asking the Lord to set the people free to follow Him. I will not go into the details of what happened during this time of prayer except to say that it involved intense struggle in spiritual warfare against the forces of darkness. The battle was so severe that I had to cut short the prayer to five days only. At the end of this time, I went to the front door and stretched out my hands to heaven and said to the Lord, "Here am I. Send me!"

Chacko and Radha with Sheela and Sunil on board the Logos II sailing up a river to Santa Fe Argentina in1993.

Chacko and two of the OM ship staff in front of the Logos II in Santa Fe, Argentina in 1993

Chacko Thomas and family in London with friends celebrating Sunil's 17th birthday in 2002, nine months before he passed away.

Back on Doulos in Asia

I received a call from Dale Rhoton, the general director for the OM ships, within that week. He was based in Germany. This was around November of 1989. It was nearly seven years since I left the OM ships, in March1983. He asked me to rejoin the Doulos, as someone with my gifting was needed on the Doulos. The ship was based in Asia. I made an initial visit to the ship in Fiji and stayed for one more port, Tonga. Radha and I were open to the idea, but everyone else except two Singaporeans advised us against it. Even Sheela, who was eight years old, was against it. I felt I should not go without her agreement.

There were numerous reasons for not going to the Doulos. During my fasting and prayer, I had prayed for my permanent residence in Singapore and it was approved. One of the elders in Zion Church thought this was an indication from the Lord that I should stay in Singapore. In addition, there were strands of thought within the denomination that would make it difficult for my church to support me to go back to OM. The health of the children, especially Sunil appeared not good enough to uproot again. Besides, Sheela was in a good school. It was very difficult for her to get into the school, and the school had warned us that if we were to leave, her place would not be kept for her when we came back. Radha's parents were upset. They felt I was destroying their grandchildren's future. But I had asked the Lord to "send me" and this call had come through.

We had paid a down payment for a small HDB flat. Such flats have been built by the Singapore government to make available affordable flats for all Singaporeans. We thought it would take years to get it, as had been the case with others. But it came almost immediately. Much work had to be done on the flat to make it fit to live in and the renovation had to be done within six months or else you lose the flat. Zion's missions co-ordinator, Mrs Emily Quek, assured us that she would take care of it, and would do all the work necessary within my budget. Emily has been a huge help to us ever since. Every church needs a missions co-ordinator like her. Her husband is the best missionary the church has although he is a fulltime professional. He is what I call a missionary disguised as an architect.

Meanwhile Sheela had a change of mind with no pressure from me (I was away on the ship) or from Radha. On the last week of February1990, Radha, Sheela (8), Sunil (4) and I left for the Doulos. What a risk! What a price to pay! From the posh Singapore Changi airport we landed on the grass runway of the Madang airport in Papua New Guinea (PNG). I remember Sheela looking around and asking, "Where is the airport?" She did not see anything apart from a small wooden hut where we picked up our suitcases. A van from the Doulos took us to the ship, which was docked nearby.

God confirmed that we were in His will. Amazingly, we sailed to most of the countries I had prayed for. And I was seeing the Lord set free many souls for His kingdom. I became the ship's unofficial evangelist and had lots of opportunities to urge many to respond positively to God's call for salvation in Christ. I appreciated the opportunity to serve alongside many nationalities on board. I think the biggest group at that time were the Filipinos. Thus, we began our three years on Doulos, visiting 16 countries and 58 ports. Our first port Madang was known as the Mosquito capital of the world. But the Lord protected us.

However, we had a scary start. Both children were affected by asthma. We did not sleep the first night on board. I stayed up all night on the ship deck with Sheela on my shoulders and Radha was in the cabin with Sunil. The first few days I kept saying to Radha, "we have made a mistake." I would have been embarrassed if we had to return and face her family and the church back in Singapore. But the gracious Lord intervened in answer to prayer. I shall never forget that prayer night when Bernd Gülker, the director, called on the ship brethren to pray for our children. They improved week by week, and the Lord gradually healed them from Asthma. They were both released from their asthma within the year. Thank God they enjoyed the ship life.

How to Find God. The Lord led me to start an evangelistic seminar called: "How to Find God". It was four hours long, consisting of four sessions - about God, Man, Christ and Salvation. It was publicised in an appropriate manner and tailored for the countries we visited - Buddhists, Catholics etc. The Lord used it to bring many hundreds to Him.

I remember one of these seminars in the Philippines. At the end of the seminar many raised their hands to indicate their faith in the Lord Jesus Christ for their salvation. We asked people to stay back for more fellowship and the Doulos people fanned out among the people, forming small groups. I noticed a man in deep thought. I walked towards him and greeted him. He responded, "now I know why Christ died." Just about everyone in the Philippines, being a Catholic country, knows about the death of Christ, but many of them do not know its meaning and significance. Many people in most of the countries in Asia do not even know about the death of Christ.

Indonesia opens its door. It was a joy to be back in Indonesia for a return visit to the country. I think it was the ship's first return visit since 1974. Both the ports we visited (Ambon and Bitung) were Christian areas. We had considerable freedom for ministry, but these were the only two ports in the world where the Ministry of Religious Affairs had their men present in all our conferences and seminars. It made me aware of the pressures Christians had to live with in Indonesia.

Sunil had had his fifth birthday on the Doulos in Ambon, Indonesia in June 1990. He was thrilled with 300 people singing "Happy Birthday" to him in the ship's dining room. He thoroughly enjoyed it. Then he went all over the ship and asked different ones whether they sang for him. Some of them were not present and did not know about it. So he got them to sing. For Sunil's birthday, we bought him a bicycle. Whereas Sheela picked up cycling within the first few minutes of teaching her, Sunil made me run behind him for six months. Once he nearly went over the quay side while trying to learn cycling by the side of the ship. After six months, when I was about to give up, he got it, and since then, he loved to cycle - whereas Sheela never took to cycling much.

Study medicine. One day I was standing by the ship's clinic and a young Swiss girl, probably in her late teens, asked me, "what would you suggest – should I continue with the ship or go back to my studies?" When I learnt that she could study medicine, I suggested that she should do so. Years went by, and one day I received a gift from her with a note that she had completed her studies and had started to work. She has been supporting me since. She has also served the Lord short term in several third world mission hospitals. Together with her husband and daughter, she is now serving the Lord in a Muslim land, using her medical skills.

Read Psalm 103. Another time Sunil (age 6) was standing by the same clinic when a young American came out from the clinic, with bandages on his right hand. Sunil asked him, "What happened to you?" The young man replied, "Sunil, I was so angry I hit the bulkhead of the ship." Sunil responded, "I think you need to read Psalm 103." The young man subsequently told me he did read Psalm 103 and it did help him. We had read Psalm 103 the day before during our family time, and did so again that morning because Sunil showed interest in it when I read it.

The Philippines We enjoyed several visits to the Philippines. Ever since the Logos first visited the Philippines in 1972, whenever OM ships visited the country, we have been given a warm welcome together with a door wide open for the ship ministry. During our visit this time to the island of Mindanao, which has a Muslim majority, I was invited to preach in an evangelistic meeting organised by a Christian group in the University. The young people had been fasting and praying for this event, each of them praying specifically for a particular person to be saved. At the invitation to come forward to receive Christ, I was surprised to see them coming forward two by two, and one of the two had tears in their eyes. I learned the one with tears had been praying for the salvation of the other; they were tears of joy. 41 students and a lecturer came to the Lord.

Grenade attack and God's gracious undertaking. The ship then moved on to Zambuanga, another port in Mindanao. 10 August 1991 will be remembered for the attack on us by Muslim fanatics in Zambuanga. God in His sovereign grace and mercy limited the extent of the casualties they intended to inflict on the Doulos people. The Lord led me to stop the children from taking part in this port programme, even though it meant disappointing my son who was looking forward to his role in it. However the fanatics managed to kill two Doulos people and injure 38. Thank God none of the 35 children were hurt.

This is what happened. We had come to the end of a great visit to Zambuanga. The programmes were well received by both Christians and the non-Christians. The Christians were encouraged and strengthened. Many people heard the Gospel and many thousands of Christian and educational books were sold. Only one main event remained in the programme. This was the grand finale called the International Night. It was our way of thanking the people of the city we visited, and it was also a last opportunity to clearly present the Gospel.

Close to a hundred ship people participated in the International Night, at which we presented cultural items from various countries, including mimes, songs, testimonies and a drama with a short closing message. Well over a thousand people were sitting in a large shed, not far from the ship. Large numbers had come from far and near, because we had announced the meeting on local radio as well as in the churches. In God's providence, we had to change the venue twice. The first venue was an old outdoor stadium. It was not safe. The second was the ground outside the Municipal Hall, in the open, where thousands could stand to see and hear. Our carpenters had built a strong stage, large enough for 20 people to perform a drama which presents the Gospel very clearly. This venue had been made known all over the city and to the people visiting the ship.

On the day of the International Night, the Lord sent thick and dark clouds over Zambuanga, and we were sure there would be a heavy downpour. The organisers sought permission to move the meeting into a huge terminal building, which was actually a long shed but big enough to hold a thousand people. The change in venue was announced over the radio. A temporary stage (platform) was set up in minutes, with the flags of the various countries represented on the ship hanging down from a long wire - for decoration as well as to separate the stage from the backstage. We had a full house for the meeting. The captain and a few older people sat on one side of the stage, while the majority of the ship people sat behind the stage and ready to come up for their part of the programme.

I had sensed that something might go wrong that night and that was why I stopped the children from being there. When Radha woke me up from a nap in the afternoon and told me that the venue for the International Night had been moved from an open space to a shed, I remarked to her, "How would the people escape if they have to?" What I had expected was gun shots aimed at the preacher.

However, everything went as normal. I was given the privilege of giving the short Gospel message at the end of the evening. The Holy Spirit gave our people an unusual urge to pray while I went forward to preach. They were praying in twos and threes at the back of the stage. As I got on the stage and stood between two light bulbs to preach, one of the bulbs fused. So I moved closer to the other pole with the bulb at my right. Although I was not conscious of it at that time, this shift in position meant I was now right in front of the thickest of the flags hanging from the wire behind me. I preached a message I had preached in many port cities, one which would be easier for Roman Catholics identify with: "Five Wounds of Christ".

The message was based on Isaiah 53:5 which talks about Christ being wounded in His body for our sins. Christ died for us, in our place so that we can go free and live for Him. I had finished the message and was preparing to give an invitation to follow Christ. At that moment, I heard a "pop" sound, like someone opening a bottle. I had no clue it was a grenade. In fact they had thrown two grenades. One fell right in the middle of the ship people in prayer behind the stage, killing two young ladies (an Australian and a Swede) both 18 years of age. It also wounded 38 others, some of them very seriously. The other grenade brushed past the captain's shoulder, leaving a little mark below his left ear, and fell in front of him. It then moved on, turned right and finally came to a halt under the stage where I was standing. But it did not explode.

Immediately the people dispersed. Thank God the shed was only enclosed with half walls, so the people could jump out. Everyone rapidly moved into action, including the police. The seriously injured were hospitalised while the others were treated on the ship itself. Remarkably, of the several qualified nurses who participated in the programme, none was injured. Actually one of the nurses, Margaret Gülker, the wife of the director, had been unwell for a few days. However, she suddenly felt healed, and soon after that she heard the paging over the loud speaker system on the ship asking for all nurses to come to the main meeting room where the injured were brought in for treatment. Thankfully the ship's medical clinic had all the things necessary for the care of the wounded.

The news spread rapidly. The news of the attack was broadcasted in the Philippines and the news reached many parts of the world very quickly. It was reported in the newspapers and heard over the radios in the cars and homes. A friend told me he heard the news at home in Texas, USA, as he woke up in the morning - and all he could do was pray. That was the best thing to do. Parents, family, friends and the churches of our people on the Doulos were getting wind of the news and were deeply concerned. The ship's information (reception) counter had to be reinforced to manage all the calls that were coming in. This was before the days of mobile phones. Newspaper and radio journalists in many countries, especially in Sweden and Australia, the countries of the two girls who died in the attack, were keen to get the news as it unfolded. OM offices had to be kept abreast of the news as many were calling the nearest OM office about their members serving on board the ship. This is to be expected when you have more than 40 nationalities on board.

My brother was shocked when he picked up his newspaper in India and saw the words "Explosion on the Gospel Ship". But the subtitle relieved him: "The Malayali escaped miraculously" - Malayali is a person who speaks Malayalam, the language of the Indian state of Kerala, where I am from. A Christian newspaper in Kerala, with a large circulation among the Malayalese all over the world, carried a lengthy article giving my story and all about my parents, the church, OM ships and Operation Mobilisation. My brother quickly informed my sister living in another state in north India. But he was not at peace till he heard from me.

Fawzia Abd Elnour from Sudan was the most prepared for the eventualities. While in her cabin she had heard a voice in her ears say "prepare a bag". She turned to her roommate and asked, "What do you think it is? Is this of the Lord or from the devil?" Anyway, she prepared a bag to take to the meeting. Later, when the participants were praying together on the ship for the event, Fawzia again heard a voice saying to her, "You will not die. You will live." She was among the more seriously injured. Her jugular vein was cut and her liver, hands and legs were injured. She bled so much that she lay in a pool of blood. The ship's dentist used his finger and pressed on her jugular vein all the way to the hospital. Otherwise she would have bled to death before she got to the hospital.

A member of staff at the hospital, seeing her condition, concluded Fawzia would not be able to survive and pulled a sheet over her head. However, one of our American ladies who was nearby, pulled the sheet back and insisted that she be examined, and they did. A doctor came by, and having inspected Fawzia said, "Your chances are 50/50." Fawzia replied, "No, I will not die, I will live." Then she lifted up her eyes and saw on the wall part of a verse from John 2:4: "My time has not yet come". When the injured were being airlifted to Manila, the pilot knowing her serious condition refused to have Fawzia in the plane until the Doulos doctor signed a paper taking full responsibility for her. Well, within a few weeks, she was with the group that returned to the ship from Manila, alive and recovering. Amazingly, Fawzia survived and is active with OM in the UK.

Many grenades Subsequently, the police found five grenades in a toilet which looked down at the stage of the venue where we wanted to have the meeting – those grenades intended for throwing at the ship people had been prepared in advance. It is a miracle that only one of the grenades went off. The fact I was not even scratched was interesting. I had been no more than eight feet away from where the grenade exploded. The police found that the thick flag which hung behind me was full of shrapnel holes. They concluded that the nails that would have hit me were sent up to the ceiling by the flag behind me. That flag took all my wounds. It impacted me again that, like that flag, the Lord Jesus took what was due to me and was wounded on my behalf.

Process of recovery. The army in Zambuanga advised us to have the wounded treated in Manila, which had better hospital facilities and was further away from the militants. The next day, about 14 of the seriously wounded were airlifted to Manila, including my secretary Lynn McKane from Northern Ireland. The rest of us on the Doulos were escorted by the Philippines' Navy to Tawau in East Malaysia. A few weeks later, the group in Manila rejoined the ship. All of them survived and were recovering. I must say that Bernd Gülker, the ship's director, was at his best in leading the ship during those difficult days. We were thankful to the Lord that several of the leaders, the essential crew needed to sail the ship, the nurses and the doctor, were not hurt at all. George Barathan went with the injured to Manila and he handled the media people who came to the hospital.

A missionary psychiatrist from London was flown out to the ship in Tawau to counsel the ship people. She found most of us were resilient, especially the wounded. Some took a while to get over the trauma. There were those who would experience fright whenever there was the loud closing of a door. I remember preaching in an evangelistic meeting and when the time came to give an invitation I had asked the people to close their eyes - and then I realised I was afraid to close my own eyes - in case a grenade went off. At another meeting, a child's balloon went off in the vicinity and I was shocked.

Dr. James Hudson Taylor III, the grandson of the founder of China Inland Mission (now known as OMF), was its director then. He visited us at the request of George Verwer. Instead of telling us how sorry he was for us, he told us his story. He had been a youngster in China during the Japanese invasion. He was taken prisoner of war together with a school full of children and teachers, including Eric Liddell (of the film "Chariots of Fire"). His stories were most helpful. We felt a sense of fellowship with those who had suffered for the sake of the Gospel, and we were glad we could suffer for the sake of Him who suffered, shed His blood and died for us.

There was a brother on board who had a nasty cut on his upper arm. He did not want the Filipinos to treat him. He had the ship's doctor and nurses do the first aid on him and took the next plane back to his home country. There he was admitted to a hospital and a team of medical staff came to treat him – they were led by a Filipino doctor! God does have a sense of humour. The brother was glad to be back on the ship soon after.

The many Filipinos on board were very sad that this attack happened in their country but we encouraged them by pointing out it was not the act of the whole nation but a few misled people. After a long break, the Doulos enjoyed return visits to the Philippines. The Philippines is a leading Christian nation for missions. Her people are penetrating countries relatively resistant to the Gospel, serving as "tent making" missionaries. It is the only Christian nation in Asia. OM Philippines seeks to send out workers through the OM world as well as being part of a team helping Filipinos who go abroad for work. About 150 evangelical Christians leave the Philippines daily for jobs overseas - to places like Japan.

Turning Points

Three months of ministry in Western Australia. The winter of 1991 was spent in beautiful and peaceful Western Australia. It was their summer time. This was just what the ship people needed after Zambuanga – being in a place where we would be free from the fear of attack. It was the most refreshing three months of my life on an OM ship.

Soon the ministry momentum picked up. Besides Western Australia, we were ministering into the Solomon Islands, PNG, Taiwan, Hong Kong, South Korea, and even up into Vladivostok, Russia, on the Asian end of the continent. Many thought that the attack on the ship people resulting in the loss of two lives and injuring many would mean a significant fall in the number of new recruits for the Doulos. We were wrong. For the next year, there were more recruits than usual for the ships, and among them was the sister of Karen Goldsworthy, one of the teenage martyrs.

A George Verwer visit to the Doulos. It took place in Darwin, Australia in December 1991. Usually a George Verwer visit to an OM field would be like that of a typhoon - it blows apart all your neat plans. We were approaching the end of our two year commitment to Doulos and I told Radha that we had better have our plans in place. We informed our family and church back in Singapore that we would be there soon. We had been praying that the Lord would put Sheela back in to the good school she was in before we joined the Doulos, and that Sunil would be accepted into a good school.

Bernd Gülker, the director of the Doulos wanted me to host George Verwer on the ship and I did this with my secretary, who followed it up. We were blessed by his three-day visit. He met up with many ship people one by one, besides speaking to us as a team on a number of occasions. I don't remember the ship ever "closing down" for the visit of its founder – but we nearly did that on this occasion – so that he could have many sessions with us. There was a sign-up list of ship people to see him. I was not on the list. On the third night, George's last night on board, the telephone rang in our cabin, just before we would have gone to bed. George Verwer wanted a brief time with Radha and me, in our cabin. We had a good, short chat and I updated him on our plans. He expressed regret that I had made my plans without hearing him. He had hoped that I would move on to the OM ship Logos II to be its director. We prayed and he left. I felt I had won the day.

The next day, after long sessions with the ship people as a team, it was time for George to leave. The telephone rang. George Barathan, whom I had put in charge of sending George to the airport, told me that George wanted my name on the list of people going to the airport. Well, at the airport George was busy talking to the people one by one. I was there to say goodbye. Just before his time to go, my turn came and George talked to me about the need for a director for the Logos II. I promised to pray about it. Knowing this position could easily be filled, I said to George, "If no one is found in the next six months, let me know, I will do it." "Do you know what you just said?" asked George. "You said, 'yes' – because there is no one when Mark leaves after his year of commitment." That was only eight months away.

I was the next director of Logos II by September 1992. Our children never went back to Singapore to study. I became the first director of an OM ship who was not a Caucasian. Until then, there had been several Americans, a couple of British, a couple of Germans plus one Australian. Since my time, we have had a Singaporean (Lawrence Tong), a South Korean (Daniel Chae) and a South African Indian (Seelen Govander) as directors for the OM ships.

George has a keen eye for people who are at the crossroads and matches them with gaps in the ministry. One of his secretaries had a screen saver that read: "God loves you and George Verwer has a plan for your life". Thank you George. Missions need people who can "call" people into action, like Jesus called His disciples. I have never seen anyone as skilled at it as George. We Christians are sometimes better at "star gazing, like the apostles looking into the sky" – something I had heard George say – like the disciples in Acts 1. May the Lord send his angels to dismiss them.

A friend of mine from England had been serving on the Logos and with OM in India for many years. He was a very able person, and did much for the literature ministry of OM wherever he was based. One day he felt that his time with OM was up. He wanted to move on. He went and spoke to his country leader, who consented. They then prayed together and said goodbye. He had officially left OM. He then went to George Verwer to announce his leaving but he came out of George's office in 15 minutes with a new job description and a huge stack of books. He was back in OM. He served the Lord in very satisfying ways till the Lord took him home at age 52. That was my first OM funeral. Philip Morris's service to OM India is nearly unmatched. Thanks to God and to George Verwer.

Radha's Birthday and Sheela's cake. Doulos was back in PNG where we had joined the ship nearly two years earlier. We were in the port of Rabaul, famous for its volcano. Radha's birthday present from me was a drive and a hike up the huge volcano early in the morning of 25th January. It was the morning after an all night mission prayer meeting on board for the PNG believers in the Rabaul area. A few local believers joined us as guides. Sunil came with us, but Sheela who was 10, did not join us as she had to attend the ship school. We were back on the ship by about 9am and Sheela had gone to school. As we entered our cabin, we were pleasantly surprised by the smell of freshly baked cake. Sheela had, all by herself, baked a lovely cake in our little kitchenette in the cabin, by following a recipe! She had also thoroughly cleaned up the kitchen before going to school. Thank God nothing caught fire! Wow! I wonder if the captain ever found out. Sheela also made my 60th birthday cake - this time with icing and all the rest.

The biggest church in the city It is a joy to see PNG missionaries now serving the Lord in various places including France and Sri Lanka. PNG was famous for its head-hunters. Now they are going after men for the Lord Jesus. A great part of the country has turned to the Lord. One Sunday morning, in the Port of Lae, I believe, I was scheduled to preach in the biggest church in the city which was attended by many dignitaries. So I imagined a big building. The pick up for the team came in a nice car, confirming my expectation. But then I saw we were driving away from the city. It turned out that they met in a park under some huge trees. Worshipping God in this way, in the midst of His creation, was an experience to be remembered. It also brings home the truth that the church is the gathering of God's people and not the building. However, it is helpful to have a place for meeting if we can afford it.

Taiwan. After a wonderful ministry in PNG, the ship sailed towards Taiwan. We had a brief ministry in the little island port of Koror in Palau and then visited two ports on the beautiful island of Taiwan in the spring, arriving in April. One youth meeting has stayed with me. It was a large evangelistic meeting. Throughout the day I had sensed that an intense spiritual battle was going on. Being Saturday and holiday time for the children, I decided to go for a drive with Radha and the children before heading back for the evening meeting. I ended up spending most that "holiday" on the roadside with a broken-down van, and subsequently in a workshop getting the van repaired. At the meeting, it was a blessing to see 50 Buddhist young people give their heart to the Lord. It was an answer to much prayer and fasting together with the simple Gospel message and exercising authority over the forces of darkness. The evil one will not let go of those in bondage to him without a fight. Taiwan was one of the countries I prayed for while back in Singapore.

Taiwan is a beautiful country, with people who go out of their way in the practice of hospitality. For a break, we stayed in the home of an elderly, bed ridden Christian lady. She has planted 49 churches during her lifetime in Taiwan. Her helper, taking very loving care of her including occasionally taking her for a drive, included us in it all. I remember visiting a hot water spring. I had never seen one before. Our family visit to the Taipei Zoo was the best – the zoo was very spacious and had a wide range of animals, birds and reptiles. I was also on a land team to Hua-lien on the east cost. The drive along the beautiful mountainous coast was breathtaking. The ship enjoyed a great visit to Taiwan, with huge crowds that came to the book exhibition.

By the end of April 1992, four months after the chat with George at the airport in Darwin, there was only one thing lacking in the process of appointing me as the director of the Logos II. That was for me to visit the ship and see it for myself, its people and its ministry – partly because the director, Mark Dimond would have finished his commitment by the time I was able to join the ship with my family. His commitment and that of the directors before him was only a year each. Not the best arrangement for the team on the ship. Radha and I could only commit ourselves to two years as our children had to be placed in a school on land by then - although the ship schooling is of a very high standard. Our daughter was already 10 years old and our son 6. The longer we waited the harder it would be for them to fit into schools in Singapore. We were already taking a huge risk with the children's welfare.

Two weeks with Logos II. At that time the Logos II was in Ecuador, on the west coast of Latin America. The ship would be in Latin America and the Caribbean for the two years we were asked to serve on board. So I spent about two weeks on board the Logos II in Guayaquil, Ecuador in May 1992. My task was to move the ship from refit mode to ministry and training mode. There were many hidden needs. The ship had more than a few "old matrons" who insisted on the style of "hospital" in which the ship ought to be run. It was also a time for the ship people to meet me. I knew less than a handful of them. The personnel manager and the chief engineer together with their wives were old hands going back to the Logos. The chief engineer, Dave Thomas was among the original crew of the Logos, and had served under George Verwer, the first director.

On the physical side, although just as spacious as Doulos for ministry (fitted with large meeting rooms and book exhibition area), the setback was the staff accommodation. Whereas the Doulos was formerly a luxury liner, the Logos II was an old car ferry, which OM bought and re-fitted with cabins and the ministry area. It was alright for single people and married couples but not suitable for families. Only the captain, the chief engineer and the chief Officer had an attached shower and toilet. Everyone else had to go the communal toilets and shower rooms. The dining room that seated 200 people were very noisy when they came together for meals three times a day. For older people this was difficult. By faith I committed to join in September, when the current director completed his commitment and returned to the OM Ships Headquarters in Germany.

God encouraged me during this visit. One of the visitors to the ship recognised me from my last visit to Guayaquil in the early 80s with the Doulos. He introduced himself to me as one who was saved in one of my open air meetings in town. He was a drug addict, with nothing to live for. He heard the Gospel message but did not make a decision when I urged the crowd to do so. However, he could not sleep that night - my face appeared before his mind several times. Finally at midnight he got up and prayed to the Lord Jesus Christ. He told me he felt at that time he "had nothing to lose, but now I have everything to live for." He was then a pastor, having completed his theological studies and was a member of the local committee for the ship's visit.

Back to Doulos in Korea. I rejoined my family and the Doulos in Inchon, South Korea where the ship was beginning a three month visit. The Logos had visited the country several times and I had the joy of having been there once before with the Logos. It was great to fly into Korea at night, seeing thousands of crosses in red and blue neon lights on top of church buildings. I have never seen anything like this anywhere else.

What a great country South Korea is. Little over a hundred years ago they had no churches. Now one third of the country is Christian and it has some of the largest churches in the world. About 40 years ago there was hardly a mission vision there, but today it is the second major missionary sending nation in the world after the USA. The Korean language has the second largest number of Christian book titles in the world – only the English language has more. It is remarkable what this praying nation has accomplished.

OM South Korea is one of the fruits of the Logos visits. It is one of the more significant OM fields and for several months it assisted the line-up for the ship ministry. Rev Stephen Choi was the national director. During a briefing between the Doulos and OM South Korea staff, which was the first meeting of the visit, director Bernd Gülker said that he would "shortly be leaving the ship for a long break in Germany. Chacko Thomas, the associate Director would be the acting director for the time the ship is in Korea." The OM Korea leader replied quietly "We in Korea don't like acting directors, we only like directors."

Since Bernd and Margaret and the Gülker children needed to go for a well-earned break from the ship, it was decided that from the start to the end of the ship visit Chacko would be the director. Stehen Choi and I were able to serve together like brothers during the ten weeks the Doulos was there. South Korea is not the place for one to learn to be the main director. It is a job for the initiated because it is a country with many formalities and traditions. But God's grace and the prayers of many helped me and the ship people. The ship's team rose to the challenge. After all, we had come to serve them.

I was blessed with able leaders to assist me, and I especially remember the programme manager Dave Hoffman, a young American. We visited all the main ports of the country: Inchon (serving the capital Seoul), Mokpo, Yosu, Cheju, Pusan and Pohang, from May - July. Our main message to the Korean church was that the Great commission was also a Korean obligation - not just the responsibility of believers from the West. It is interesting that a mission challenge should come from an Indian - although there were dozens of other speakers from many countries on the ship.

The long visit to S. Korea was more intensive than any country we had visited. I had to be in my full suit and tie from the time I got up until the time I went to bed and that was usually after a huge meal in a Korean restaurant with dozens of ship and local Christian leaders or dignitaries. Our people enjoyed much hospitality and the generosity of the believers. We had an unscheduled day-off for the whole ship in the middle of the visit, with a BBQ on the beautiful quayside of the Maritime University. It was here I met up with Gim Su Yong. He later accepted the invitation to serve as the chief officer of Logos II, and is currently serving as the OM Director for Korea.

To Russia with love. The next port of call was nearby. I had never even heard of Vladivostok in eastern Russia till we started to pray for this place during the ship's weekly prayer nights. George Barathan and his team had started to line up the programme. This would be the first ever visit of an OM ship to Russia (although the Logos had visited communist China about ten years earlier). God was opening the way in spite of the tight security of Vladivostok – it was one of Russia's large navy ports with lots of navy ships of all sizes and more than a few submarines.

We had been announcing the Russia visit to all the churches and conferences on board in all the Korean ports. A project "love pack" was introduced to the Korean churches - to donate a large bagful of clothes, food items etc, to give to our brothers and sisters in Vladivostok - for their own use and also for them to pass on to others. Some 6000 large bags full of "love packs," most of them weighing nearly 10kg, were generously given by the Koreans in the six ports. They were collected and stored in the ship's hold - enough to fill five huge ship containers.

The Lord gave us a great two weeks in Vladivostok, one of the few countries where I spent a lot more time on shore than usual. I enjoyed distributing tracts in the city centre, not too far from the beautiful berth given to the ship. It took the ship two full days to transport all the 'love packs' to a Baptist church, from where they were distributed to local believers. The main events here, as far as I can remember, were the Book Exhibition and evangelism in the open. We were mindful not to overdo it in a newly opened-up communist country.

This was my first experience of visiting a communist country, except for driving through Yugoslavia about fifteen years earlier. It is interesting to note how the political and religious environment of a country affect its people – whether it be communism, democracy, or the religious influence of Islam, Hinduism, Buddhism or Christianity. Christianity can survive and even triumph in all kinds of environments. However we find it in Europe, where secularism combines with materialism, we have one the most deadly and least conducive of environments for the growth and health of the church.

Nagasaki, Japan the next port of call for the Doulos was also the last port for the Thomas family. Our family did some sightseeing and I had a few meetings, but most of the time was taken up with packing and saying good bye to people. However, I shall not forget an evangelistic meeting on shore, where 12 people came to the Lord. Japan was one of the countries I had prayed for and it was a joy to have a part in seeing a few turn to Him. We did our 'How to find God' seminars, but the result was minimal. One man told me he believed in science, not in God.

This country needs a spiritual breakthrough which only prayers and evangelism can accomplish. The church in Japan is too small to impact the nation. It needs wise personnel, well-suited for the Japanese mindset and Holy Spirit empowered input from the rest of the world, alongside the church in Japan, to witness to the truth of the Gospel in a way the people can understand and appreciate. Let us cry out to the Lord for workers for the harvest field of Japan (Matthew 9:37-38). Oh, what would be the impact of an evangelised Japan on our world!! They make great missionaries.

The Family Joins
Logos II in Latin America

Well, instead of heading for Singapore as I had firmly decided before George Verwer arrived on board the Doulos in Darwin, Sheela (10), Sunil (7), Radha and I now headed for the Logos II in Colombia, South America. We journeyed from Japan – Singapore – London – Columbia. But we were wiser (for once), having stopped over in each place for a few days, unlike our straight flight to Jamaica in 1982.

The short stop in Singapore for time with the family and the church was vital, as our move to the Logos II meant we would be away for another two years in South America and the Caribbean. I can never be too thankful for the support I have in Singapore, especially from the family and the mission minded church. The stopover in London was to see George Verwer for any last minute instructions. The only thing I can remember from that visit is his words to me as we parted: "Be in maximum contact." We enjoyed a good break in the West Watch "mansion", temporarily given for OM International's use for leadership meetings and trainings, not too far from George Verwer's residence.

On board the Logos II. I was glad to be in South America again. Our first port was Barranquilla in Colombia. I was thankful to have the chief officer's cabin. The chief officer had a cabin in a different section (family section) of the ship, from where he could look after the safety of the ship, the main hazard being fire. We had our own attached shower and toilet facilities and Radha even fixed up a little kitchenette in the space available. This was helpful for the young family and kept the Singapore tastes alive. The cabin was smaller than the one we had left on the Doulos, of course. It was a family living room during the day and a bedroom at night, with a pull-out sofa bed. Both Sheela and Sunil were given a cabin each, in spite of the shortage of space on the ship. Sunil's cabin, the biggest of the three, served as storage space for the family. This was our home for the next 25 months.

Here are the ports we visited during this period

Barranquilla, Colombia	Sep 21st - Oct 20th 1992
Cartagena, Colombia	Oct 20th - Dec 10th 1992
Maracaibo, Venezuela	Dec 12th - Dec 28th 1992
Santo Domingo, Dominican Republic	Dec 30th - Feb 1st 1993
San Juan, Puerto Rico	Feb 2nd - Feb 23rd 1993
Ponce, Puerto Rico	Feb 24th - Mar 9th 1993
La Guairá, Venezuela	Mar 11th - Mar 31st 1993
Puerto Cabello, Venezuela	Apr 1st - Apr 20th 1993
Puerto La Cruz, Venezuela	Apr 21st - May 11th 1993
Cumana, Venezuela	May 12th - May 25th 1993
St George's, Grenada	May 28th - Jun 7th 1993
Bridgetown, Barbados	Jun 9th - Jun 22nd 1993
Georgetown, Guyana	Jul 2nd - Jul 13th 1993
Paramaribo, Suriname	Jul 14th - Jul 26th 1993
La Plata, Argentina	Aug 14th - Aug 31st 1993
Buenos Aires, Argentina	Sep 1st - Sep 22nd 1993
Rosario, Argentina	Sep 23rd - Oct 3rd 1993
Santa Fe, Argentina	Oct 13th - Oct 26th 1993
San Nicolas, Argentina	Oct 27th - Nov 7th 1993
Montevideo, Uruguay	Nov 10th - Nov 28th 1993
Puerto Madryn, Argentina	Dec 16th - Jan 1st 1994
Necochea, Argentina	Jan 4th - Jan 25th 1994
Mar Del Plata, Argentina	Jan 27th - Feb 16th 1994
Bahia Blanca, Argentina	Feb 18th - Mar 7th 1994
Porto Alegre, Brazil	Mar 12th - Apr 5th 1994
Santos, Brazil	Apr 8th - Apr 25th 1994

Vitoria, Brazil	Apr 27th - May 16th 1994
Salvador, Brazil	May 18th - Jun 6th 1994
Bridgetown, Barbados	Jun 17th - Jul 5th 1994
Castries, Saint Lucia	Jul 6th - Jul 26th 1994
Kingstown, Saint Vincent	Jul 26th - Aug 2nd 1994
St George's, Grenada	Aug 3rd - Aug 15th 1994
Port of Spain - Trinidad,	Aug 16th Sep 12th 1994
Scarborough, Trinidad and Tobago	Sep 13th - Sep 19th 1994
Gibraltar, Gibraltar	Oct 6th - Oct 17th 1994
Toulon, France	Oct 21st - Nov 1st 1994

A changeover on the Bridge. I had just been on Logos II a few days when the new captain, Tage Benson, along with his wife Marta (both Swedish), came to take over the ship from Tom Dyer (American). We gave a great send-off to Tom and Maggie Dyer. Tom was known in the OM ship circles as "Typhoon Tom" because of the number of stormy seas through which he had to manage the ship. Captain Tage Benson (63) was much older than Tom, and had served OM ships, on and off, since the days of the Logos. I appreciated the experience, both on ships and in OM, which he brought into the ministry of the Logos II. However, we had not met before on the OM ships and it was a new working relationship.

Changes in personnel. There were a number of changes to the ship's senior personnel, including the change of director with me coming in. Soon, we had a new programme manager, associate director, programme coordinator, line-up coordinator, PA to the director and other new personnel. I became the Director just before the main annual changeover period of OM. Thank God for the things that do not change, especially our faithful Lord and His Word.

The day the captain arrived with his wife, the air-conditioning on the ship failed because the river water had so much industrial waste in it. Our engineers worked round the clock to fix it, but it still took time. The ship became a hot oven, as most of the portholes on the Logos II could not be opened. The problem was aggravated by the fact that we were in the hot tropics. Although the captain had the biggest and best cabin on the ship, he did not want his wife who had spent most of her life in Sweden, to go through the ordeal. As we were in port, the personnel director, Em Namuco, arranged for them to stay in an air-conditioned hotel, with the captain coming in daily to work onboard. Soon the air-conditioning was fixed - to the relief of all on board.

Refitting Logos II. The Logos II had been built around 1968 and we only had about six months lay up period instead of a year to convert it from a car ferry into a passenger ship. We needed accommodation for 199 crew and staff, and facilities for the large book exhibition and for meetings of up to 400 people on board. Thousands of volunteers worked on the engine, deck and steward departments. It was "rough and ready" enough for the ship to sail and minister while simultaneously carrying on with the rest of the renovation. Hundreds of volunteer workers were coming and going every week from many industrialised nations to re-fit the ship. The ministry facilities were fantastic.

From work mode to ministry mode. Much work had to be done over the next few years, and you could always hear banging away on the metal or carpentry work all around the ship. There was also the never ending job of chipping away the rust and repainting the ship. Work on an OM ship will never end. It costs huge sums of money to lay-up and repair the ship professionally in a dry dock, and we try to minimise that. Besides, OM is a movement big on redeeming the time. It has become a habit for some, with a few workaholics around. OM seems to attract such people, action people, especially to the ships. It must be the influence of the founder, although George would deny he is a workaholic. Once he told me, "I am not a workaholic, but just that I have a passion for what I am doing." Praise the Lord!

"You are here to work" was what our people were told. It was understandable in the first few years, but it was time that ministry and training were moved to the front burner. This was more so in Latin America where the demand for the ministry of the ship was so huge. Besides, the recruits to the ship were sent by their families and churches for ministry and training. This was what we promised when we recruited them. I remember one day I had to tell that "the ship does not exist for the engine room" and the one concerned accepted it graciously. The change had begun, and without a major strain in relationships.

However, it is not always easy for a big community in a confined space of ship, with the many different personalities, nationalities, denominations, age groups, social and economic backgrounds, to work together in harmony. Thank God for His gracious and sovereign undertaking - He is the One to whom we all sought to submit to. I cannot say that I handled all things in the best way possible. In fact, I am painfully aware of some of my failures.

A good team There were many things to be thankful for. The leadership, in God's providence, was becoming strong. Peter Nicoll, the associate Director, was a young but experienced pastor from South Africa, with a strong ministry of the Word. Em Namuco from the Philippines had been with all three OM ships for many years and he was the personnel manager. Assisting him with matters affecting single women was Ruth Tomlinson from South Africa. John Satterly from England was the Book exhibition manager, a good leader of people, with a great vision for literature ministry. Marty Banzhaf, a young American was the training manager. He was highly motivated in training people and was assisted by his Peruvian wife, a former missionary to Brazil. These brethren were of the right age for the average ship people - most of them were in their late teens and twenties.

Duane and Margaret Grasman. One day, David Hicks, the OM USA director told me that "I have an American who has been with OM in Mexico for many years and both he and his wife are fluent in Spanish. He has the gift of an evangelist and is great with young people. They would benefit from a short break from Mexico. They are happy to do evangelism all day every day." This couple was exactly the kind of people I would like to have for the ship. It seemed absurd to me to be running an evangelistic ship and yet be deficient in evangelists. Although I had the heart of an evangelist, much of my time was taken up with work on board with the ship people and with conferences. And here was a brother who could go out every day, leading evangelistic teams of ship people. He was also a trainer of people in evangelism.

But there was a space problem. They had three children, which would mean the whole family would take up three cabins - the children taking up two cabins which could accommodate four much needed adults in the work force. On the plus side, their children would be a blessing to the dozen or so children on board. I decided to "bite the bullet". It seemed to me a good investment for the ship ministry.

Duane and Margaret Grasman and family joined Logos II and bonded well with the ship people, particularly with the Latin brethren. He also preached in Spanish with great impact on the conferences on board. When the position for the programme manager became vacant, the ideal person to fill it was Duane. Duane was very reluctant to accept the invitation to do so but I am glad he did. It was good for the ship and the countries we visited. About two years later, Duane became the first OM Latin American area leader, one of the dozen or so area leaders of OM International.

PA for the Director. Soon, there was a vacancy for a PA to the director and I placed the matter before the Lord. The personnel department was on the lookout but they could not find anyone on the ship interested in it. In desperation I pulled out the personnel list and went through the front page and most of the back page, but could not think of anyone who could be a possibility. Most were needed where they were serving already. Then, near the end of the list, I saw the name Vomhof, Christina. I told myself it would be great if she could assist me.

Christina was a young German lady, leading the kindergarten on the ship. Children loved her and so did their parents. I thought I would never be able to get her out of that role. Besides, why would a kindergarten teacher want to become a PA? I talked to the associate personnel manager Ruth Tomlinson. Ruth approached Christina. As it turned out, having been on the ship for a year, which was half way through her two year commitment, Christina was looking for a change.

Christina fulfilled her role well, although it was not easy for her to be the link between me and the ship people. It was good to have a European secretary, as the majority of the ship people were from Europe or USA. Smiley Christina was what George Verwer would call "a happy camper". She laughed when I told her that I felt like "a chicken with its head cut off". This may well explain my style of leadership.

Once I delegated a difficult job to her. I wanted the Logos II to present the Gospel message more clearly and with greater enthusiasm as I was not comfortable with "pussy footing" types of evangelism in countries that were wide open to the Gospel. The Doulos had incorporated drama into its Gospel presentations and they drew many into God's kingdom. I wanted the same on Logos II. You may wonder, "What is the problem with that?" Well, none of us are exempt from the universal spirit of "we have never done it like this before" and "what is wrong with what we already have?" The idea was opposed from the start by a few who would have to accept it to make it happen from port to port.

I was determined to push ahead with the idea, and invited a German friend who was leaving the Doulos (having completed his term) to come over to the Logos II for two weeks to train about 20 people for this drama. It is a powerful drama that tells the story from creation, the fall, to Christ – His life, death and resurrection and the second coming - and our joyful reunion in heaven. It takes about 40 minutes to perform it.

Christina had to get people released from the different departments on the ship for the training, and these departments were always short of people. But she managed it well, between the department heads and the people themselves, who had to give up their short breaks. After a week or so, the group was ready to perform in public. But I had been informed that this programme would not be accepted on Logos II.

It was Thursday night - the ship's weekly extended time of prayer. Usually our prayer meetings were strictly prayer times, with more prayer and less talk. I decided to take 40 minutes to show this drama during the prayer meeting, which was attended by most of the ship people. To my own surprise, the brethren performed the drama superbly. Of special note was the way the Brazilian Jefferson Nascimento Da Silva played the part of Christ's death and resurrection.

It was very moving. Most of us were in tears. To give people time to absorb what they had seen and felt, I announced a short break before we proceeded with the prayer time. The brethren fanned out in all directions on the ship, some silent, others weeping, and all very appreciative. I stood by a rail looking out into the darkness on the water side, wondering how I could get this drama accepted into the ship programme. Just then, the person in charge of that section came by and told me, "We will use this drama in the programme." And the Lord used it in every port as part of the ship's International nights, to draw many to faith. I often had the joy of giving a short evangelistic conclusion after the presentation of the drama, and then giving the invitation to those present to receive Christ. Thank God for the hundreds who have indicated their decision to follow the Lord after these meetings.

Christina produced a weekly newsletter, keeping the ship company informed of happenings on board and in OM circles. There were arrivals and departures of people at just about every port as well as announcements from the department heads, birthdays etc to report. She took to writing like a duck to water. One of her jobs included taking down the planning meeting minutes. Once she told me that my job was like her dad's - he was the mayor of a German town for most of his life. When her year ended on the ship, Christina joined the ships headquarters in Germany, serving with the head of the personnel department. Now she is happily married and serving a local church and I believe she is doing the church's weekly bulletin.

My first Planning meeting on the Logos II. The planning meeting is made up of the director (who leads it), the captain and the department heads - the chief engineer, chief officer, chief steward, chief purser, book exhibition manager, programme manager, line-up coordinator, the personnel and associate personnel manager. Being my first meeting with them, I had fellowship at the top of my mind. And what a time of fellowship we had!

Usually the first person to present items for discussion is the captain. And the captain said, "I want to discuss the blue strip." I knew it was trouble. The ship was painted all white at the refitting in Holland. It was the idea of the man in charge of the refit. He was a skilful and diligent chief engineer but he was not really big into consultation. He had been on the Logos II project right from the beginning, and had poured out tons of sweat into turning what many called a "rust bucket" into a beautiful OM ship. Three years later, someone had suggested that the all white paint be broken by adding a blue strip of paint that goes round the ship. The deck people then added a beautiful blue strip of paint from the bow of the ship all the way to the back and it broke the all white look. Most people thought it made the ship look better. They also added a broader stripe of blue paint going around the bridge section of the ship. However, the chief engineer had the ship restored to its original all white look.

And now, the captain wants to discuss the matter, or rather he wanted the blue strip of paint put back! Thankfully God undertook, and without too much discussion or sparks, we were able to settle to have it the captain's way (and that of the majority on the ship). It stayed that way till the end of the Logos II and it made her look beautiful. The way the matter was resolved resulted in greater mutual respect between the deck and engine departments, and enabled the deck department to get on with their work. It was good for the ministry of the ship.

Wake up calls in Barranquilla, Colombia. This was where our family joined the Logos II, and right from the start, I was aware that we would be confronting the strongholds of the evil one. I had one or two dreams which made me think of it and I concluded that it may have something to do with the spiritual forces of witchcraft and idol worship so prevalent in that part of the world. For the next 25 months on the Logos II, the Lord helped me to do something that I had never done before or since. I would get up whenever I woke up at night, usually between 2 and 3am. Everyone on the ship would be fast asleep except a handful of night watchmen in the engine room and on the deck. When we were sailing, a few more would be around on duty with the officers on the Bridge and the Engine room and I would enjoy hours of prayer walk on the quay side, walking back and forth the length of the ship. I could not have led the ship without this time with the Lord - time to think and pray. It must have done my body some good too - walking has become my favourite exercise.

The dreams alone would not have got me walking and praying so early in the morning. During the first days on board, I had noticed an old ship out at anchor, a long way away from us. It could have been there for months. One day, to my horror, I saw that ship going up in flames. A few days later, I saw an ambulance come to the quayside at the back of the Logos II to receive a few burn victims from another ship further down the river. Apparently there had been an explosion in the engine room in that ship. Several things went through my mind. I knew we could not take anything for granted. We must cover everything in prayer - "We wrestle not against flesh and blood..." (Ephesians 6:12).

A Korean Chief Officer. The ship's office in Mosbach, Germany had been looking for a chief officer to replace the Dutch officer who was coming to the end of his time on board. Early one morning I went to my office to have my quiet time, and on the way out I happened to see a fax to me from Mosbach, saying there was no chief officer available for Logos II. While I was in the shower and praying about it, Gim Su Yong came to my mind. I had met him in Korea a few months ago. I faxed Mosbach asking them to contact Su Yong. Mosbach managed to contact his wife who said, "He has gone to the prayer mountain to pray." When he came back from the prayer mountain, we learned that he had been waiting on God for His will for the next step. They joined the Logos II for several years. The captain and the chief Officer worked well together, and the Captain and Marta were like grandparents to the Gim children. Such working relationships are priceless. Su Yong today is the director of OM South Korea, serving a second term.

Latin leadership. The ship is a good platform for leadership training, especially on the job training. There were 43 leadership positions on board, big and small. However, on closer examination of the Logos II leadership, it became clear that more than half of the leaders came from one country and most of the others from one or two closely related countries. Latin leadership was absent. It would be good to have an international leadership, representative of the ship people. Since we were in Latin America, it would be helpful to have some of them in leadership positions.

Duane Grasman was a flexible programme manger. One of his section heads, Fernando Garcia from Mexico joined the planning meeting as Line-up Manager. While the ship was in a port ministering, there would be preparations going on in upcoming ports for the ship's future visits. The Line-up Coordinator oversees this group of people and liaises with the ship. Fernando served on the Logos II for several years, and now he is the director of OM Mexico. God did put together an International leadership team on the Logos II for Latin America that worked. Others who were brought in by the Lord included Brazilian 1st and 2nd engineers.

Argentina. Logos II visited nine ports in the long strip of land that is Argentina. It took us six months from August 1993 – February 1994. The main emphasis of the ship visits was mission mobilisation. I sought to have a good working relationship between the ship and the OM field in the countries we visited. Daniel Bianchi who had been with OM since the first visit of the Doulos, was the national leader of OM Argentina. He was given a cabin on board so that he could come and stay on board, especially at the beginning of each port visit, so that he could meet with the local committees and be at the official opening of the ship in each port. He was also present at the end of the port visit to meet with the local committee and ship leaders for a port evaluation. Being a great speaker, he was also involved in all the main meetings on board including the pastors' conferences.

The Miracle of a rising river. The Lord who dried up the Red Sea and the river Jordan could also raise up the water level in the river for the Logos II to sail up to a new port. This was in early October 1993. The ship had been going up the river, a branch of Rio Parana, the second largest river in South America, the largest being the Amazon. It was ministering in the city of Rosario. The next port city was Santa Fe. I had been there with the Doulos, a much bigger ship, some years before and we expected a similar programme. However, we learned from the line-up team that for some years now, the water level of the river had been going down. No ship the size of Logos II had been up that way for a few years.

Fernando Garcia who lined up this port for the Logos II recalled: "We had only 2.3 meters of water and the ship needed 5.4 meters to sail into the port. We could see fish dying because of the lack of water in the river and the captain wanted to cancel the visit to Santa Fe. We were very sad. Together with the local pastors, we agreed to fast and pray and ask the Lord to give us rain so that the water level in the river would rise. The next day the rain started to fall and we saw the miracle of the river rising to the level needful for the ship."

On board the Logos II, we were also praying about this matter. The final decision was in the hands of the captain. It was an interesting phenomenon. Although there was no cloud or rain anywhere near the ship, the water level was rising daily. It could be due to a heavy downpour in Paraguay or Brazil. However, the water level had to be adequate for the ship to go up the river and to come down again after the two week programme in Santa Fe. The captain, by faith, made the decision to sail up to Santa Fe, with the full backing of the planning meeting. Many local pilots were on board instead of the normal one or two, because they wanted to experience this special trip up to Santa Fe.

All of us were thankful to the Lord for making this voyage possible. The journey up the river began without any trouble. Most of the brethren who were on the deck to witness the start of the journey had gone back to their duties. Our children were in their classes. Dale Rhoton, the general director of OM ships based in Germany was visiting, and Radha and I were entertaining him in our cabin. There was Dale on a chair facing the back of the ship, and Radha and I were facing the right side of the ship, with no worries in the world, enjoying the calm cruise. Everything was normal for a couple of hours. Suddenly we felt a jerk - the bottom of the ship was scraping against the sand at the bottom of the river, and the ship came to a halt. We looked at one another, not sure what to think. We just prayed and stayed out of the way of the captain. It took our captain about an hour to wriggle the ship out of that sand bank and resume the journey. We learned later that the pilot was over confident and wanted to take a short cut across the bend, rather than stay the course where he knew for sure the water was deep.

There was great rejoicing when the ship arrived in Santa Fe. The Lord gave us a great programme. Fernando recalls, "When the ship came in there were hundreds of people on the berth to welcome her. Even the port administrator was there, and he said truly this was God's ship because he saw how the river rose. A few weeks earlier, he had said only God could bring the Logos II into the port. That was the best visit of the whole country. Thousands of people visited the ship - the highest number of visitors for the country - and the book sales were very high."

At the end of the programme, we were glad to see that we had the water needed to sail down the river to San Nicolas. There was a huge crowd on the quayside to say goodbye. Many of them were local volunteers from the different churches in the city who had laboured alongside with us on board during the two weeks. This was Fernando's last line up with me. He was promoted to become the line-up coordinator of the Logos II ministry and it was good to have another Latin American on the main leadership team.

George Verwer visits Logos II The ship was in Georgetown, Guyana. I had completed a year on board, with a little more than a year to go before we would head back to Singapore with the children, to put them back into the Singapore school system. This had again been in my daily prayers. We were concerned about how Sheela and Sunil would fit into the Singapore school system after having followed the British system with excellent teachers, mostly British and Americans. George Verwer, who happened to be in that region, spent a couple of days on the Logos II. This was his first visit since I took over Logos II as director. The ship people, as usual, enjoyed his ministry.

It was great that George was on board as this also was the port where we said goodbye to our chief engineer (perhaps the longest serving chief engineer on OM ships) and his wife and daughter. I tried my best to retain Dave, Joy and Heather on the ship but I was not successful. One of my motives was that his daughter Heather and my daughter were of the same age and got along well. Besides Joy, his wife was doing so much with the two girls, from teaching in the Sunday school to cross-stitch and other crafts.

George has known Dave from the beginning of the Logos ministry as Dave was among the original crew of 43, as the second engineer. As the family walked down the gangway, George broke out in tears and disappeared from the crowd. Dave and family joined OM UK, served as its director for six years. Of course, you could not keep him away from sea. Dave and Joy gave another 8 years to OM ships (2000 -2008) before the Lord called him home to Himself.

Now, George's question to me was, "What do you plan to do after the Logos II?" I replied in the same way as before, "go back to Singapore and, get the children into the school system there, and seek the Lord for the next step." Going back to Singapore did not sound to George like what God had been training me for. George suggested that I join him as the associate team leader of his International Coordinating Team (ICT) in London, U.K. He wanted a two year commitment.

The ICT had about 50 people at that time. George was still the international director of OM.. The ICT was made up of many senior OMers who were looking after many ministry aspects of the work. The associate team leader, Mike Wakely, together with his wife Kerstin were returning to lead the OM work in Pakistan. Mike had started the OM work in Pakistan, but had to return to the UK because of the children's schooling. The children having left the nest, he was free to return long term to Pakistan. George needed a leader who would stay with the team in London, especially because he travelled a lot.

Being in the West was never an attraction for me. The only attractive thing about this offer was that my children could continue in the British education system. I said to myself, "all these years the children have followed me, it is time I followed them." My wife was in favour of the idea and I had another year to prepare myself for London and the UK. So without even doing any home work, I agreed to make London my next ministry base. An American friend who heard about this expressed concern: "I have the grace to work with George from 3000 miles away, but I am concerned for you if you have to work so closely with him. However, I shall be praying for you." Well, I was blessed because George was going high on grace because of the influence of Charles Swindoll's book Grace Awakening. He was distributing the book in the hundreds, if not thousands.

Logos II in Brazil. The four ports we visited in Brazil were blessed by the Lord. Humberto, the field leader of OM Brazil devoted much time to the ship's visit. He is a great speaker as well as a good singer. His ministry to the ship people was greatly appreciated. Radha, Sheela, Sunil and I were given good holidays by Humberto and Silvia. It included a visit to the famous Iguassu waterfalls where Argentina, Brazil and Paraguay meet. It is a glorious sight. I have enjoyed many return visits to preach in Brazil with OM Brazil and the churches there.

Two long voyages Some of the longest voyages I have done in 15 years on the OM ships were on Logos II. The voyage from Paramaribo, Surinam to La Plata, Argentina was 17days long and the sea was very rough for a good part of the voyage. The other long voyage was from Scarborough, Tobago (Trinidad & Tobago) to Gibraltar which took 16 days (September-October 1994). But this journey was one of the smoothest, in answer to much prayer. This was one of the last voyages for us as a family and it was a memorable one. During voyages, my son always prayed for a rough sea and I prayed for calm seas. I think most people on the ship would have preferred calm seas.

We set sail from Scarborough in normal sea conditions. Three days into the voyage the captain informed us a typhoon had developed in Trinidad and was heading in our direction. It followed us the whole way till we got to Gibraltar (near the southern tip of Spain), all the time staying two to three days behind us, allowing us to sail under high pressure air, and ensuring a calm sea for us. The captain also informed us that there was a storm developing in the West African region - it was heading north and we may run into it. This was enough to keep some of us on our knees before the Lord. As it turned out, when we approached Africa the storm had died out completely. We received news that one passenger ship went down in the cold Baltic Sea with hundreds of passengers. The Logos II arrived safely at the port in Gibraltar, and was safely tied up before the storm following us went over Gibraltar, leaving behind some destruction in its wake, and giving our officers and deck crew the difficult job of securing the ship.

Goodbye to Logos II. Gibraltar gave us a wonderful start in Europe. The second port was Toulon, France, where the Logos II and the Doulos met up, for the second or third time in the ships' history. By this time Peter Nicoll had already taken over as director of the Logos II. The OM coach came to collect all the British people returning to the UK. All our belongings in suitcases and cardboard boxes were loaded into the bus. We did not go back to Singapore.

Missionary to and from the UK

Missionary Visa for the UK. It was no small miracle that I had a Missionary Visa stamped on my Indian passport for the UK. This was how it came about. Dave Thomas (now with the Lord), a former OM UK director, who was the chief Engineer when I took over the Logos II, did all the paper work for me. He advised me to apply for the visa six months in advance. He told me this was how long it would take to process the Missionary visa application. Since such visas had to be applied for at the British embassy in one's home country, we left the ship in Barbados for Singapore, stopping over in Europe on OM business. At the British embassy in Singapore, I placed the three Singaporean passports on the top and my Indian passport at the bottom, as usual. I had expected the whole procedure would take a long time. After all, I had been told it would take six months to process my visa.

About 15 minutes later, the officer called me and asked me to pay the amount required for the visas. I did as the officer said, and he told me to come back in three days. No questions asked. No interview date set up. This was contrary to all I had expected. Three days later I turned up, expecting an interview, but I was handed the passports with the visas stamped on them. It had to be God's undertaking. He must have wanted me back on the ship instead of chasing after a visa. We retuned to the ship in Barbados four days before the end of the ministry there, and continued four more great months of ministry with the Logos II.

Entering the United Kingdom. On November 14th Radha, Sheela (just turned 13), Sunil (9) and I left Logos II in Toulon, France and flew into Gatwick airport in London, UK. We were allowed to fly rather than be on the bus which left a day earlier, because it was felt my missionary visa would probably encounter fewer problems with the immigration at the airport.

When the officer stared at our visas and began asking me questions, I thought to myself we may be getting into difficulties. Just then I turned and looked at the counter to my left and saw an OM area leader Dennis Wright, an American. I greeted him and I told the officer at my counter that he is one of the main leaders of OM, the organisation I would be serving with based in England. Dennis later told me that he "sensed that our meeting at the immigration counter had some significance". Yes, it did. Although it took time for the immigration procedures, Gary Dean who came to pick us up, waited patiently at the pick up point. He prayed as he waited for us. Finally we showed up.

We arrived during one of the coldest winters for years. Of the four of us, I took the longest to adjust to the weather, the culture and everything else. Dennis and Carol Clifford who oversaw the OM schools including the ones on the ships knew our children and had booked them a place each, in two different schools. Both were only a short walk from our new rented home in London. I was given a long time to settle down. It was a month before I had enough confidence to drive in London. Mike Wakely told me: "You have just stepped off a fast train so don't be in a hurry to get on the next fast train."

Joining ICT. I joined George's large International Coordinating Team as its associate team leader. Have you ever led a team of leaders? Visionary leaders? I think I was more a facilitator than a leader and I enjoyed fulfilling the responsibility. One of the commitments I had to make to George was that I would stay put in London. This would free him so that he could be away from the team and travel all over the world, as his schedule called for it. This was not a bad idea for a family which had been travelling for five years and covered 40 countries with the two ships.

The main office, 39 Honor Oak Road, Forest Hill had office rooms, a meeting room, dining room and kitchen to cater for the conferences held on the premises. Some talented team members put up some good mission displays, and a Canadian teacher who taught carpentry at school made structures for the book displays. We managed to turn an old facility into a conference centre.

The most meaningful times were the weekly prayer nights. They were very informative, with firsthand information from many mission frontlines being brought back by our team members who were constantly travelling - especially George. We tried to disseminate the information to others by organising events like India day, Algeria day, Pakistan day etc. Many leadership and mission events also took place, making the most of George's availability as well as other key people on the team. There was a big display of books available for the public to buy books at "George Verwer's discount". People were always leaving the meeting place with bags full of books.

Children and schooling. Sheela got into a well reputed school. She did well in all subjects, excelling in maths, which gained her recognition in school and the whole country among her age group. However, there were things that shocked her as well as us. Her background was on the two missionary ships, which had daily prayers twice a day, and a preacher for a father. Sheela was a happy Christian but she was never exposed to the outside world. One day she came home and asked, "What is a lesbian?" Apparently a couple of the teachers were lesbians. Soon she learnt that her precious faith was frowned upon. And she went all quiet about being a Christian.

I was very concerned but all I could do was to pray with Radha over the whole matter. We also kept up our family prayer time daily, and we prayed with the children when sending them to school. One day Sheela told us she didn't want to join us for prayer. I was very disheartened, although I didn't show it. I knew she should not be

185

compelled. Moreover, we were not in India where the father's word is the law and the emphasis is on the community rather than on the rights of the individual. Here in UK, it is at the other extreme, with emphasis on the rights of the individual rather than the community.

Thankfully, God was at work, and He kept Sheela's faith. She eventually went to London School of Theology (London Bible College), and she is now serving the Lord. It is not easy to be a believer in the UK where the Christian faith is ridiculed daily in the TV and the press. Please pray for the UK and Europe, where Christian values and practices are gradually being eroded.

Sunil was clear about where he stood. He could not be bothered by the constant ridiculing of the Bible and the truth of the Christian faith. He was not intimidated, even by big names. He used to watch documentaries on nature and to him everything was created by God, even though most of the programmes were based on the assumption that evolution is true.

He was very active in the weekly Christian meetings at school. He managed to get his religious education teacher to buy 40 Bibles for the class to use. He got along very well with his arts teacher which worried me because the arts teacher was an atheist and mixed up in New Age thought. One day Sunil asked me, "Dad, what book do we have to give to an atheist?" I showed him the book "Show me God" and he gave it to his teacher. His sincere faith was contagious. His response to any problem was to ask me to pray about it. He prayed about it too. He would never miss the church service, even when unwell. More than once I picked him up from the hospital, which allowed him to be away for a few hours so that he could go to church.

Staying on. We were committed for two years, but George asked me to stay on, and we have stayed on ever since. The fact that I was in the UK, as required by my job, helped me get a British passport - in the fifth year of our being here. After prayer and discussion with George, I took up British citizenship which enables me to carry out an international itinerant work with the many open doors the Lord has been giving me. I must confess there was a deep pain in my heart when I had to surrender my Indian passport and citizenship. I was in tears. This period in the UK also gave me time to do some studies which the Lord has been using in my preaching and teaching ministry - especially to Hindu, Muslim and Buddhist new converts and those ministering to them.

Seven years into leading the team in London, I felt I needed to pass the job to someone else. More than that, I had personal health issues and Sunil was seriously ill, suffering from cancer. After a long search to find a replacement for me, I recruited Kenny Gan to assist George. Besides looking after Sunil with Radha and Sheela, the Lord was opening new doors and reopening an old ministry I had in Bible teaching. The first call came from Yusuf in Algeria, North Africa, to "come and teach the book of Romans". A year later, I was able to teach the book of Galatians in Algeria. All my 90 students for the Romans studies and the 70 for the Galatians studies were Muslim background believers. What a privilege! There are many thousands of them in Algeria. God has been opening doors into many countries, some of them I never got to visit with the OM ships. And some of them in those parts of the world where the young church is growing very fast and in need of Bible teaching ministry.

A deposit in heaven

On March 7, 2003 the Lord decided to call Sunil home to Himself. He had suffered much. It is very painful even to recall it. There is an essay he wrote for his class work, which is entitled "The worst day in my life". I cannot read it. Just recalling it is very painful. Many thousands prayed for us. But God, instead of healing him, gave him power from on high to go through it. What a cross he had to carry, but how cheerfully. The Lord also gave grace to Sheela, Radha and me to go through this period. Here is what he wrote. It is the last assignment Sunil did for the school coursework, from hospital. He was given good marks for it. The teacher's comments are given below.

THE WORST DAY IN MY LIFE (by Sunil Thomas)

The 18th of May 2001, stands out as the worst day so far in my life. I had been quite ill and was admitted to Kings College hospital for 8 days before, since the 11th of May undergoing various tests and surgical procedures.

That morning I was rudely awakened by the "vampire nurses" for their four hourly blood sample collections and also for taking my temperature and my blood pressure. I had little sleep that night as I was still in much pain from the biopsy of the previous day done on my neck and shoulders. Worst still, was my lower back where they had operated to take a sample of bone marrow tissue. In fact my arms and even my groins were covered with puncture marks and scars from unsuccessful attempts at drawing blood and trying to insert the canula. So you can imagine the agony that I had endured. The codeine they gave had no chance to work because the babies around me kept wailing all night like banshees as it was a paediatric ward. Besides that the oxy-meter attached to my toes kept bleeping at the slightest turn.

Breakfast was disgusting as usual, the cold toast and jam, which I could not stomach. My mum forced on me a small bottle of yoghurt drink. I looked and felt terrible as I was being pumped with saline solution, which the doctor insisted was necessary to flush my kidneys. All my liquid intake and output had to be measured and recorded. How bothersome and inconvenient!

I was too miserable and tired and did not bother with the horde of doctors, consultant, registrars and medical students who invaded my room on their ward rounds. I heard them muttering something to my mum.

Later that morning the haematologist, Dr. Height came and sat on my bed and wanted to talk to me. I knew something was serious. She explained it in great detail, but I only heard the word lymphoma – a type of cancer called "Hodgkin's Disease".

At first it did not sink in and I complained to her about my various aches and pains especially the increasing pain in my shoulder. She tried to reassure that an X-ray and an ultrasound would be done before my transfer to Middlesex Hospital.

Suddenly learning about my diagnosis and transfer to an unknown hospital hit me hard. I became terrified and panicked and burst into tears as this was all too much to bear. My parents tried to console me but to no avail. I began to imagine I would die.

Sleep would have comforted me of my miserable state. However this was not to be, as the radiographer barged in with the cumbersome x-ray machine for yet another chest x-ray. Soon the ultrasound equipment rolled in accompanied by a moody technician. He applied some disgusting goo all over my bloated torso and began to prod and poke, increasing misery. When I cried in pain, he ignored me, adding insult to injury. I was told that the fluid in my chest cavity caused the excruciating pain. I wish I could curl up and die except I couldn't curl up because I was so stiff and sore.

The nurse brought my medical reports and informed me that the ambulance was waiting to take me to the Middlesex Hospital. It was a big struggle to get me out of my bed and onto a narrow ambulance stretcher.

The ambulance ride was another ordeal. My bladder was full and about to burst as I was being pumped with fluid intravenously. I was in pain and the London traffic was horrendous.

After what seemed like hours I arrived at the Middlesex Hospital. It looked grey and daunting and I cried and insisted on being sent home. I was scared as I was wheeled to the Adolescent Unit. Some teenagers in wheelchairs stared at me. It was an open ward and I was put right in front of the nurse's station so that they could watch me closely.

Dinnertime was over, so there was nothing to eat except cheese and crackers. By this time I was all puffed up like a toad with all the fluid. My mum was worried and reported it to the nurses. A doctor soon came to see me and ordered the fluid to be reduced. Still I did not feel any different.

It had to be the exhaustion, discomfort and all the upheaval of the day that made me feel so wretched and full of self pity. I felt life was unfair. I already had epilepsy, asthma, dyspraxia and now Hodgkin's Disease. I could not hold back my tears.

The night nurse, Chris, was kind and understanding. She brought a VCR along with the tape Matilda and a bowl of sweet popcorn. Some friends brought some Tesco's chicken dinner, which helped me forget that I had to take a small cupful of chemo tablets. This was how that terrible day ended."

The teacher's comments: "What can I say, Sunil? Thank you for sharing these experiences with me! An excellent piece of coursework! Detailed with good use of vocabulary throughout!"

The prayers of thousands were not wasted. God's abundant grace was upon Sunil as he went through this very difficult last phase of his life on earth. We also learned a lot through it and heaven has become more real and nearer to us. I did not realise that the Bible had so much to say about heaven. The Lord Jesus has made the last enemy, death, a servant to bring us to the doors of heaven. I look forward to heaven and the long list of people I will meet. It may not be an exaggeration to say that I think of heaven daily.

Sunil was honoured by his church CRC, especially the Per Svensson family, and by his school, Langley Park School for Boys. A new wing to the school building was named "The Sunil Centre", in recognition of his contribution to the arts department of the school. His suffering and death was a "teenage triumph", a rebuke to the devil who attacked him so severely. There were articles written on him, which the Lord is still using. One of them by Debbie Meroff, the OM writer, reported on the Funeral service with the caption: "A Celebration of Sunil." I wrote one entitled: "I have come to help you die". Both of these are produced below.

A CELEBRATION OF SUNIL (by Debbie Meroff)

London. March 14th. The little church was packed to the doors, with many people standing: Next-door neighbours, church friends, classmates and teachers, three nurses who had cared for him, OMers and former OMers. Young and old, they came from nearby, from all over the United Kingdom, and as far as Germany. They gathered to remember a 17-year-old boy whose brief life had touched them all in a special way.

Sunil Thomas would have been surprised and pleased by the tributes. Younger students at the Langley Park School for Boys had asked their Headmaster if the flag could be flown at half mast that Friday, and so it was. Sunil's fellow-Sixth-Formers were not required to attend the service, but they decided they wanted to be there. So did several of Sunil's teachers, the head of the Board of Governors, the school's Assistant Headmaster and the Headmaster himself, who asked if he could say a few words.

After reading a poem by Sunil that reflected the teenager's great love of animals, he mentioned Sunil's gift in the area of art, noting that his work was part of a travelling exhibition to other schools. "In his GCSE year, out of almost 200 students only one was awarded the highest prize: Sunil. Life was never easy for Sunil. He was diagnosed with, dyspraxia, Aspergers Syndrome, epilepsy, and Hodgkin's lymphoma. But he brought out the best in us all - pupils and staff - just by knowing him." The Head ended by announcing that a new addition to Langley Park School would soon accommodate autistic students. They had decided to name the new building in Sunil's honour: "The Sunil Centre".

Representatives of OM India and OM Ships also spoke of Sunil's impact on his world--the love and laughter that he gave so many, his commitment to Jesus, his refusal ever to complain. Pastor Gabriel Yee commented, "Sunil was taken when he was only 17. But many of us in our 50's and even 60's are still struggling to love the way Sunil loved."

Vera Zabramski, OM team member and "buddy" of Sunil added, "By the world's standards he was disadvantaged but that didn't stop him from enjoying life. And he had an unshakeable faith. Once he told me he didn't like a particular TV wildlife programme presenter because he was an atheist. 'How can you not believe in God,' he cried, 'when He made so many wonderful things?'"

OM's International Coordinator and Associate Coordinator, Peter Maiden and George Verwer, also shared. "Sunil has been part of God's plan to help change me--to be more like Jesus," said George, with emotion. "It's not how long you live, it's the quality of your life."

Radha's brother, who spoke on behalf of the family, and the men from the small church that Sunil so much loved refused to allow

Sunil age 9, just before leaving Logos II to London

Sunil, a year before his promotion to glory

professional funeral staff-strangers--to shoulder his casket, and took the responsibility themselves. A large number went on from the memorial to accompany Chacko, Radha and Sheela to the committal service, at nearby Beckenham Cemetery; then they returned to the OM office--to share further remembrances of Sunil, and marvel at the samples of his artwork on display.

Sunil's love of eagles was very evident in those paintings. The day before the Lord took him, he had fulfilled a 4 year-cherished dream to see the Stellar Sea eagles in a distant Birds of Prey centre. As he sat watching them in his wheelchair, perhaps these words came to him, the words sung today at the celebration of his young life:

Hold me close, let Your love surround me!
Bring me near, draw me to Your side.
And as I wait, I'll rise up like the eagle,
And I will soar with You,
Your Spirit leads me on,
In the power of Your love.

You're free at last, Sunil. Soar on.--Until we meet again!

Debbie Meroff
Operation Mobilisation "

A week after his passing away, I felt led to put my thoughts on paper. God has been pleased to bless many through this piece of writing. Though Sunil is no longer with us he is still speaking. He is still a missionary for the Lord.

I have come to help you die (By Chacko Thomas)

It was with great sadness that we laid to rest the body of our 17-year-old son, Sunil, at Beckenham Cemetery in London, England. He had been fighting a cancer called Hodgkin's lymphoma for over two years. We were thankful for each day he was alive, especially when we saw that we were fighting a losing battle. Sunil has successfully beaten his parents and his older sister to the finish line. He was promoted to glory on the 7th of March 2003.

Literally, thousands of people all over the world prayed fervently for his healing. I do not know anyone else for whom so much prayer and even fasting have gone up. Surely, the Lord would heal him? There were some "prophecies" and even "dreams" shared with us to that effect. But that was not what happened. I even wondered if I had failed the Lord and thwarted His "will" for a miraculous healing because of my sins or unbelief.

The main answer to prayer was that Sunil's own faith and ours remained strong to the end, even though it was severely challenged. Though the Lord did not heal him, He poured out His grace, which was more than sufficient for us. God also richly made provision for many of Sunil's wishes to be fulfilled. His cherished wish to see his grandmother in Singapore was arranged soon after the doctors in the Teenage Cancer Unit in London told us that there was nothing more to be done medically. He spent the next two months with her and took in the sights and tastes of Singapore in spite of being wheelchair bound. The events he enjoyed most were the two visits to the Night Safari Park, Christmas and New Year with our church, and the Chinese New Year celebrations in China Town.

Halfway through the visit we learned from the Singapore doctors that Sunil might not have more than four months left. Soon after that he insisted that he wanted to return to his home and friends in London. This was made possible through the generosity of many good friends. One particular Christian family in London put themselves at his service. Among other things they drove him around the country, to the London Aquarium, the Marwell Animal Park and the Birds of Prey Sanctuary, fulfilling a longing he'd had for four years.

We had no plans for the day after the visit to the sanctuary. We'd been out the whole day, a round trip of 240 miles, and all of us were tired. But just to give Sunil something to look forward to I promised a ride in the car as I was leaving for the office at 7.00am. When I returned home at 11.30am he had already gotten his mother to arrange a visit to his school at 2.30pm, 30 minutes before it closed. I will not take time here to explain what a marvellous reception he had at the school from teachers and staff.

Little did we realise that this would be the final day of Sunil's life. We knew that he was weak and his breathing was laboured. When we got home, the hospice nurse was waiting for us, and soon there was a visit from the local doctor. After examining Sunil she told us he was doing very poorly, and advised us to send for his sister, Sheela, who was attending a counselling course about two hours away. That night at 9.54pm, 30 minutes after Sheela arrived, Sunil entered the Lord's presence as we prayed together. The next few days were unbearable. We could not control our tears, for we have never loved anyone more deeply than we loved Sunil.

Our hope for miraculous healing was shattered. Many had encouraged us to keep believing and praying for a miracle. I had read many Scripture portions during those many months which I thought were pointing towards God's miraculous intervention. We were half expecting it up till the last minute, even while seeing his condition worsen month by month.

"We prepare our children for a long life", implying not for death, wrote a mother in an account of her teenage son's promotion to glory. An issue that came often to my mind was: "how I could have better prepared my son for death". How does a father, who wants his seventeen-year-old son to outlive him, tell him that he may not recover and that he must be prepared to die? In my role as a father I tried to give Sunil hope and courage, though I will not take credit for the strength he showed in death. But should we not do more, especially parents, pastors and fellow-believers?

I remember our pastor in Singapore coming to me after a service and saying that he had chosen a particular song with Sunil in mind. I assured him the whole service was appropriate for him. There was enough there to make us all look forward to meeting the Lord. God had other ways of preparing Sunil, too.

One thing I did when the opportunity came was to preach in our local church. I chose to speak lovingly on 1 Thessalonians 4:15-18 about "the Christian hope of resurrection". I remember a month later driving with Sunil and singing,

"Heaven is a wonderful place, filled with glory and grace. I want to see my Saviour's face! Heaven is a wonderful place."

However, I am afraid that most of my Scripture readings with the family were to strengthen our faith for healing and living, rather than to prepare my son to die. I remember an email from Ron Penny, who had lost a one-week-old granddaughter just weeks before. He wrote: "Don't just look upward, look forward", implying that we should look forward to the hope before us, to be with Christ.

About three weeks before Sunil passed away I was at my desk. Looking up, I saw on the bookshelf a book a friend had given me when Sunil was first diagnosed with cancer. It was entitled, "Will God Heal Me?" The book did not interest me then because the answer was obvious: God heals, which meant God will heal my son, God will hear me especially when I fast and persist in prayer. After all, I have seen so many answers to prayer. I had let the book remain there for two years. Now, however, I needed some hope. Flipping through its back pages, the title of a chapter called "I have come to help you die" caught my attention.

This chapter told the story of a young lady who had come to the end of her life. Reality was going the opposite direction of all prophecies and dreams and visions that various others had been given about her. Unlike my situation, visitors and prayers were diminishing as the once-enthusiastic prayer supporters saw her condition deteriorating. Then a minister went to see her.

"Have you come to pray for my healing?" asked the young lady with great expectation. Maybe the moment for the fulfilment of all predictions had come.

"No", came the pastor's answer. "I have come to help you die." The minister then turned to the many Scripture passages that speak of the Christian's hope of heaven, resurrection and eternal life. Thus she was prepared to meet the Lord, and soon afterwards she did.

I have received several hundred emails and many phone calls and visits since the Lord took Sunil to Himself. Many spoke of the fond memories they have of Sunil. Though he died young, friends assured us that he had lived a full life and finished his mission. 400 people came to the funeral service because, as one later wrote, "he had touched their lives in some way". His life did touch thousands of others in the 40 plus nations he visited with us on OM ships. This was clear from the emails that were coming in. The nine people who paid tributes at the service also made that very clear. No wonder that about 30 students and 17 teachers and staff from his school were at the service. Three of his nurses and several of our non-Christian neighbours were all present and heard the Gospel through Peter Maiden and George Verwer.

Many wondered how such a young life could be wrenched away so prematurely. Peter Maiden in his words of welcome at the service of celebration for Sunil's life said, "Christianity makes no great attempts to answer the philosophical issue of suffering. Instead, it offers to us the God of the Cross. In other words, God's answer to our suffering is to share our pain; to suffer with us, and ultimately to take all our suffering upon Himself and leave us free; as free as Sunil is this Friday morning from all pain and all suffering; and he will be free for all eternity. That's the promise of God: not immunity from suffering, not explanations for all our sufferings, but the invitation to come to Him with our pain knowing that He understands, and saying to us: 'In My Son, Jesus, I have been there; I have been where you are; I fully understand'".

A prayer by George Verwer ministered to many who questioned and some who were even frustrated that God did not heal Sunil. He prayed, "Father, we just want to have a time of thanksgiving to you and I just thank you for the life of Sunil. I would have never done it this way God but you know best. I don't like the way you operate Living God if I'm honest, but I worship you in mystery. I submit my own lostness and my own neediness to you and believe in your sovereignty and as it says in those last verses in Romans 11, we will never be your counsellor; we will never fully understand your ways but we go forward by faith…

"Lord, you have spoken today loud and clear. You have spoken through this family. So many families when they lose a young child like this, bitterness, anger, confusion and depression comes rolling in but Lord we see your grace in the Thomas family. Not that they won't experience some of these things but we believe ultimately they have that victory in you sovereign Lord Jesus. Although we greatly miss Sunil we know that he is in a far better place and what our whole ministry is about is to rescue the perishing and care for the dying. We thank you that you have saved Sunil and that he is with you for all eternity."

I cherish an email from Jonathan McRostie, an OM leader and a friend writing from his wheelchair to which he has been confined since a road accident on the mission field two decades previously. He wrote, "Recently I was at the funeral and memorial service of my own father in California. Obviously my circumstances are quite different than yours as my father was 98 and had completed a long life for the Lord; whereas your son Sunil was 17 and had a short life for the Lord. Nevertheless, the eternal life with the Lord is a great blessing for both of them! When going through some books that my father had left, I found a quotation underlined by him from the book "My Daily Meditation" by John Henry Jowett. Jowett was a British preacher in the 19th and 20th centuries. On page 81 of that book he was commenting on Revelation 22:1-6. Here is the quotation that my dad underlined in some of the last years of his life:

'And yet I must die! Yes, but the old enemy shall be my friend. He will not be my master, but my servant. He shall just be the porter, to open the door into my Father's house, into the home of unspeakable blessedness and glory. Death shall not hurt me.'" How I wish that Sunil had read these words.

Christians do not look forward to death, but look beyond death to life eternal in the presence of the Lord. The Christian's death is compared to sleep, sleeping yet alive. The Lord has come to help us to die. There is sufficient help through the teachings in God's word. The example of the Lord, in His suffering death and resurrection is a big help. No one is more prepared to die than the ones who love Him. Sunil's last words were, "I love you, Jesus". He told his mother a week before his death that he was not afraid to die, because he was going to Jesus. In spite of my failure to prepare him to die, the Lord had prepared him. Even though I walk through the valley of the shadow of death I fear no evil, for He is with me. I have heard it said that "God gives dying grace to the dying man".

We are not alone in helping our loved ones to walk through that dark valley, but we have a role. It is not easy but it is not impossible. Several said at the service for Sunil, 'It's our wish, when it's our time to go, we could go in the same spirit that Sunil did.' On the front cover of the order of service were the words of our Lord Jesus, "I am the resurrection and the life. Those who believe in me, even though they die like everyone else, will live again. They are given eternal life for believing in me and will never perish. Do you believe this?" What a hope! And what a help!

I was concerned for months how my wife and daughter would take Sunil's home going. I was relieved to hear my wife pray, "Thank you for giving Sunil to us. Thank you for taking care of him. Thank you so much for the love he has received from so many and we thank you Lord that he is safe with you and that you have taken responsibility of him. I just want to thank you for today. In Jesus' Name. Amen." She had found help to accept the Lord's decision. My daughter told me, "Soon after Sunil passed away, I looked down and saw his body and I felt someone saying, 'Sunil is not here. He is alive' ". The Lord has helped her too. Thank you Lord Jesus, for helping us all to face death.

[This article is written for the glory of God and dedicated to my son Sunil Thomas, 8 June1985 - 7 March 2003. A few weeks after his going to the Lord, a friend of my wife visited us for two weeks, and she gathered up all the stories she had heard and read about Sunil and wrote out a devotional reading for 29 days, called "Moving Moments with my Maker".]"

How many children do you have? Well, my answer still is two, one with the Lord the other with me. I hope Sunil is at the front of the welcome party Jesus puts together for me when I reach the other shore.

Healing fire. Exactly two weeks after Sunil passed away, on March 21, we were in for another shock, which could have claimed the lives of the remaining three of us. I had gone to bed very early that night. Radha had gone to bed late in another room, having taken some pain killer tablets. Sheela was very late in going to bed. All of us were fast asleep. At 1 am I was suddenly awakened by the smell of burning. On the wall in front of me I could see images of fire flashes. I quickly got up and checked, and to my horror the bathroom was on fire.

I closed the bathroom door (thanks to ship training), woke up Radha and Sheela and sent them downstairs, and dialled 999. The Fire Brigade arrived in less than 10 minutes, just as the fire was moving up towards the roof. The two teams managed to put out the fire in about 30 minutes. The smoke blackened the walls upstairs and downstairs, the bathroom was totally wrecked, and the glass in the windows shattered. Thank God nothing valuable was damaged - especially all the memories of Sunil - photos, books etc. Sunil's belongings were the only thing we talked about during the 30 minutes while we were waiting on the street as the Fire Brigade worked on the house. Thankfully nothing was lost.

The culprit was the old electrical system. The insurance refused to begin repairing the damage till we changed the wiring system. We had to move out for a few months before the repairs were done. Eventually a new bathroom was put in and the house painted. The smell of smoke and fire was somewhat gone and we moved in. Looking back, perhaps this was God's way of healing us. The house and the gardens both front and back, were so full of memories of Sunil. Being seven miles away in a flat that had no memories of Sunil for three months was God's way of healing us, although he was constantly in our thoughts, conversations, prayer and praise.

Lim Kou of Singapore. I first met Lim Kou and his wife Florence on the Logos when they joined the ship for three months in 1975. Kou is a Lawyer by training and Florence a nurse. For many years now, he has been leading a dedicated congregation known for its emphasis on the Scriptures, prayer and giving to missions. During a visit to Singapore in December 2002, we met up briefly in his flat and he showed me the draft copy of his first book "Understanding Job", subtitled "Reflections on the meaning and purpose of Job's suffering". He was going to produce it from his own pocket and give it away free. I suggested that I could help open doors and distribute them all over the world through the OM world. The last I heard, he has printed a total of 198,000 copies of this book and two other titles, The Two Kingdoms and Man of Faith. The OM ships have been one of his distributors. The three books, numerous text messages and more than 400 audio messages covering the major truths of the Christian faith are available on his website www.godandtruth.com . They can be freely downloaded for personal use or reproduced for free distribution to others.

Looking forward

Some time later, Radha and I were attending the weekly OM prayer meeting in Forest Hill, led by Kenny Gan, the team leader. Sitting behind us were George and Drena Verwer. This was unusual. George and his wife Drena usually sit on the front row. Half way through meeting, George handed me a scrap paper on which he had scribbled the words: "Minister-at-large, Special Projects, Operation Mobilisation". Well, this was to be my next role in Operation Mobilisation. George Verwer told Frank Dietz, "A minister at large is one who is fully in OM but free to follow the leading of the Holy Spirit."

God has been opening many doors for evangelism, strengthening believers, mission mobilisation, mentoring frontline-mission workers - through preaching and teaching, and one-on-one ministry. I love teaching the Books of the Bible. So far it has been the books of Genesis, Exodus, Matthew and Revelation. What joy it has been for me to teach many first generation Christians from Muslim, Hindi and Buddhist backgrounds. They are better witnesses for the Lord among their own people than I can ever be.

I have also enjoyed teaching pastors and evangelists in the 10/40 window nations. Many of them have leadership responsibilities thrust upon them even though they may not be adequately equipped - and they deeply appreciate whatever Bible teaching they could receive. I could write pages on some of the Bible conferences, Bible Schools and pastors' conferences where I was privileged to teach the Word of God. I love my new role. God knows best.

Future is as bright as the promises of God for a believer in the Lord. Only God knows what the future holds, and I look forward to it, with great anticipation. May His name be glorified; His Kingdom come and His will be done, on earth in our time, as it is in heaven.

God's ways are higher than our ways. These have been an amazing 60 years of journeying with God together with many brothers and sisters in the Lord, from so many nations. Thank you for your part in my life. I would appreciate your prayers for the days ahead. God is good!!! I am fully satisfied in the Lord Jesus. He is LORD. I am looking forward to the bright hope He has revealed in His Word for His followers. Meanwhile, may He use us for the glory of His name and the extension of His kingdom!

Romans 14:7-9 " For not one of us lives for himself, and not one dies for himself; for if we live, we live for the Lord, or if we die, we die for the Lord; therefore whether we live or die, we are the Lord's. For to this end Christ died and lived again, that He might be Lord both of the dead and of the living."

It is grace that brought me safe thus far and grace will lead me home. Lord Jesus, please grant me to finish well according to Your word in Jude 24-25 and Philippians 1:6. Your grace is sufficient. "Now unto him that is able to keep you from falling, and to present you faultless before the presence of his glory with exceeding joy, To the only wise God our Saviour, be glory and majesty, dominion and power, both now and ever. Amen." "Being confident of this very thing, that he which hath begun a good work in you will perform it until the day of Jesus Christ"

Thank you Lord Jesus,

Thank you brothers and sisters,

Further Reading:

Operation World by Jason Mandryk
Heaven is Richer by Ten Lions by Chacko Thomas
Touch of the Master by Debbie Meroff
Drops from a Leaking Tap by George Verwer
Revolution of Love and Balance by George Verwer
Hunger for Reality by George Verwer
Out of the Comfort Zone by George Verwer
No Turning Back by George Verwer
The Logos Story by Elaine Rhoton
The Doulos Story by Elaine Rhoton
Understanding Job by Lim Kou
The Two kingdoms by Lim Kou
Man of Faith by Lim Kou